Praise for What War?

"Mayan communities in Guatemala remember the government's genocidal assault of the 1980s as *la violencia*, the violence. Survivors protected themselves by a culture of silence. A middle-aged American stranger who knew little Spanish came to teach English and, somehow, encouraged young Mayan university students to share their pain-filled memories with her and with each other. This book records that extraordinary achievement."

—Staughton Lynd, peace activist, author and historian

"Until Laurie overcame the language barrier to listen with profound respect to the stories of these Mayan youth, they had not even had the opportunity to share their experiences among themselves, let alone the larger world. Their moving histories portray families with the courage and resilience of survivors determined to make a better world."

—Sue Ellen Kingsley, director/founder of Copper Country Guatemala Accompaniment Project

"These are young people who were born into a generation of violence as the Guatemalan civil war claimed the lives of family members and forced whole communities to move. The students interviewed in this volume have vivid memories of their experiences and, importantly, they were willing to share their stories with Laurie Levinger and with us, the readers of *What War?*"

—Carol Hendrickson, Ph.D., Hampshire College

"History, told through the stories of those who lived it, compels us to listen with our hearts, with compassion and a promise to be alert...alert to the suffering of the victims. The visible and invisible scars recounted in these remarkable chronicles gives us a new appreciation of the evil perpetrated in the name of government, and the incredible beauty and strength of the human character. Levinger has captured an extraordinary account of the young men and women who are working to overcome the tragedy of their childhoods. She is to be commended for listening with her heart to the unhearable."

—Charlotte Houde Quimby, MSN

"How do people survive terrible events and yet retain a sense of hope and possibility? This question echoes throughout this powerful and courageous book. When the Guatemalan civil war broke in upon their lives, most of the men and women who tell their stories here were very young…Laurie Levinger, with a therapist's skill and patience and with a sensitive outsider's eye for the beauties of another culture, encourages her conversation partners to explore their memories and to make sense of the past. As she sets these stories in their historical and sociological context, and as she draws out the larger themes embedded within them, Levinger presents a richly-textured portrait of the realities of genocidal conflict. Anyone who responds to the cry 'Never again!' must read this book."

—Susan White, PhD

"Laurie Levinger, a retired social worker, went to Guatemala with volunteers to teach English to Maya university scholarship recipients. Well-trained, intelligent, perceptive and kind, Laurie began to hear her students' life histories, how they had been affected by the violence perpetrated on their communities by the Guatemalan military. We hear Mayan voices who witnessed these events or felt the ripple effect of this hidden, rural war. These narratives are not only gripping, they tell a universal story of how even under the most terrible circumstances people manage to survive and succeed."

—Chris Lutz, Ph.D., University of Wisconsin-Madison

What War?

Saludos, liese —

laurie

What War?

....

TESTIMONIES OF MAYA SURVIVORS

LAURIE LEVINGER

RESOURCE *Publications* • Eugene, Oregon

Resource Publications
A division of Wipf and Stock Publishers
199 W 8th Ave, Suite 3
Eugene, OR 97401

What War?
Testimonies of Maya Survivors
By Levinger, Laurie E.
Copyright©2009 by Levinger, Laurie E.
ISBN 13: 978-1-61097-632-9
Publication date 8/1/2011
Previously published by Full Circle Press, 2009

Acknowledgements
....

I am grateful to many people who supported me throughout this project. First, I want to thank the Maya Educational Foundation for the opportunity to go to Guatemala as a volunteer teacher. Jane Greenberg and Eulalia Lopez came up with the idea of the English Language Program at Eulalia's kitchen table, and Armando Alfonzo from the MEF helped create the program which has meant so much to so many of us. Thanks to Bob and Jane Greenberg for their leadership of the ELP over the years.

Members of the MEF Board have been helpful in every possible way. Thanks to Chris Lutz, Carol Hendrickson, Marilyn Moors, Brenda Rosenbaum, Elisabeth Nicholson, and Susan Feinberg. Chris Lutz and Armando Alfonzo consulted regarding the history chapter. Armando has been immeasurably helpful, patient, and always available to discuss even the most basic questions. And it was he who suggested that I submit the manuscript to Editorial Cholsamaj, the Guatemalan publishers of this book.

Christine Bartlett invited me to the lunch in Antigua where I first met Balam, whose story sparked my interest in the hidden history of young Maya during the civil war. Karen Nielsen accompanied me when I returned to Guatemala to ask our students the first questions from which this book emerged.

Lucia Sebaquijay and Irma Otzoy of the Fundación para los Estudios y Profesionalización Maya (FEPMaya) in Guatemala City answered questions and offered on-going support. Through providing financial and social support FEPMaya is helping young Maya become educated and active citizens.

Bob Civiak, Marilyn Moors, and Nancy Weiss reviewed earlier versions of the manuscript. Karla Kingsley, Jeanette Fadul, Goyo Norman, and Guisela Asensio translated the *testimonios*. Guisela Asensio translated the manuscript into Spanish, asking probing questions and giving feedback that improved the book.

Susan J. White edited an earlier draft, and helped frame the chapter on religion. Her commitment to the project, her editorial skills, and intellectual rigor have resulted in a far better book than the one she first read.

Mindy Schorr, Jo-Anne Unruh, Charlotte Quimby, and Lianne Moccia witnessed the awakening of my love for Guatemala. Their interest and unwavering support have accompanied me every step of the way.

Wendy Osterweil and Eli Goldblatt endorsed the idea of this book before I'd written a word.

Thanks go to Ruth Sylvester for excellent proofreading, and to Sonja Hakala of Full Circle Press for her expertise and enthusiasm for this project.

The Anne Slade Frey Charitable Trust and the Jack and Dorothy Byrne Foundation provided generous financial assistance.

My children, Josh and Hannah, offered guidance and loving support. Martha Rockwell listened and encouraged me from the very beginning of this project.

And finally, I am eternally grateful to the students from FEP-Maya who, along with their friends and families, shared their personal war with me. I am honored by your trust.

Thank you all.

Laurie Levinger

Contents

In memory of Víctor José Pérez Pablo
who could always be counted on to tell his friends,
¡Échenle ganas muchá!

and

To all the mothers and fathers, sisters and brothers
who were victims
of the Guatemalan civil war.

. . . .

"Perhaps this is what we must learn, to collect tears and
turn them into stories. Into gestures of solidarity and compassion."
—Elie Wiesel

1
What War?

"MY FATHER WAS SHOT BY THE SOLDIERS. My mother grabbed my older brother and sister, but she could only carry two. She ran off with them, leaving me. My grandmother saved my life by hiding me under her *huipil*, and running to hide in the forest. Later, we were hunted down, the soldiers caught us and threw us in a concentration camp in the mountains...stockades in the jungle, no roof, open to the heat and rain. Mud everywhere, all the time. Hungry, I was always hungry, that's what I remember most. That's why I'm so small, so many of us didn't grow right," Balam said. "I was two years old," he added, almost an afterthought, his soft voice fading into silence.

I was standing in Balam's house in Antigua, Guatemala, when he told me these things. I'd come with a group of volunteers to teach English to Maya university students, and so far, our students were the only Guatemalans we had met. One of them had invited a couple of us to her "English professor's" home, and we had eagerly accepted. Which is how I came to be in Balam's kitchen watching him make lunch. Slim and clean-shaven, he looked like a young teenager, not the professor I'd imagined. He was twenty-four, studying international relations at the University of San Carlos in Guatemala City. He tutored English, one of the four languages he spoke. After struggling to communicate with our students, either in my limited Spanish or their beginning English, it was a relief to be able to carry on a real conversation. I wondered if I could ask Balam the questions we'd wanted to ask our students, but weren't sure we should. After all, we had come to teach English, not delve into their personal histories.

"Balam, one of the students mentioned that he was a survivor of the civil war, but he didn't say more than that. Could I ask about what happened to you, or is it too hard to talk about it?"

"Absolutely, I must talk about it," Balam said, staring straight at me. "Otherwise, it stays inside. We Maya, we look normal on the surface, we look like we're okay, but we're not really. We have to talk to get it out of us.

"Like I said, my father was killed during the war. The soldiers called all the men in our village together, and when my father understood what was happening, he tried to run. They shot him in the back."

"My grandmother was tough. In the jungle she kept asking the soldiers to let us go, she told them I was starving, that I needed food and medicine. Finally, they got disgusted with her asking, and I was so sick they were sure I would die, so they relented. 'Get out of here, you scum!' that's what they said." He demonstrated, flinging his arms like he was throwing out garbage.

"Balam, do you talk to other people about what happened?"

"A little with my friends, but most of the time people don't want to really talk about it. We tell each other stories and joke about what it was like. One of my friends was just telling me about how her family hid underground for six months. They had all sorts of games they played in the tunnels—the kids thought it was fun to play in the dirt—but they had to be quiet all the time so the soldiers wouldn't discover them.

"We need to tell what happened to us," Balam said again. "Because if we don't, when something else bad happens, like a love affair goes bad, or something like that, it all comes back, and we sink down into ourselves, and think our life isn't worth living.

"This country needs a million psychologists," he said.

· · · · · · ·

They didn't get a million, but they did get me.

But how did I come to be standing in this kitchen, hearing this horrifying tale in the first place?

The story starts, as many important stories do, in the water.

I was forced into an early retirement, when deafness made my work as a psychotherapist impossible. Untethered from my career, bereft of my identity as a helping person, I floundered. First I tried a hearing aid, followed by a writing workshop. Next came volunteering for Meals-on-Wheels, then an aqua aerobics class. Nothing seemed to really fit. I tried to convince myself that I was just wandering, remembering the J.R.R. Tolkien observation that, " Not all who wander are lost." But I wondered if, in fact, I really was lost.

Of my various attempts, the aqua aerobics class fit best, probably because I'd had a lifelong love affair with the water. At fifty-five I was the youngest of the women in various sizes and shapes who swam by, chatting amiably about food or children. It didn't matter that I never really got to know them. The pool became a destination, and my fellow swimmers became familiar faces that I paddled by three times a week. Most of the time, I only half-listened to the instructor, a seventy-five-year-old woman whose energetic commands and taut physique left me feeling dumpy and slow. I followed the others, watching, because I couldn't really distinguish their words over splashing water. One morning, during the free swim while my classmates chatted I thought I overheard a conversation about volunteering; "teaching English…Guatemala" floated by on miniwaves. I side-stroked over, "What's this all about?" They mentioned a name I recognized.

When I got home, I called. I had a million questions, but decided to come right out with my biggest concern immediately. No point in wasting time if they wouldn't let me go.

"I don't really speak Spanish very well." This was not exactly a lie, but the truth was that I'd taken just a single year of Spanish in high school forty years before. "Is that a problem?"

The silence on the other end went on a half-beat too long, just long enough for me to imagine that the man I had called was trying to figure out a nice way to reject me. "Well," he paused, "how's your English?"

"My English is pretty good." *What kind of a jokester is this guy?*

"Well, then you can come."

Which is how I came to be in Antigua four months later milling around the courtyard of our hotel, eyeing eleven other volunteers, far from the swimming pool in central Vermont: *What am I doing here?* I asked myself. *I'm not even a teacher.*

We'd signed up with the Maya Educational Foundation to teach English for two weeks. My fellow volunteers were all retired, middle-aged, white North Americans, wealthy enough to travel to Central America and pay the program fee that supported the students. Why had we come? The answers were as individual as the twelve of us standing around at 7:30 that sunny morning, waiting for the students to arrive, trying to act like we weren't nervous.

Our students were all indigenous Guatemalans, descendants of the ancient Maya. They were scholarship students, selected for their academic promise, many of them the first person in their family to attend school beyond the 3rd or 4th grade. The majority were studying law; others were students of architecture, sociology, medicine, engineering.

They arrived, the young women wearing multicolored huipiles (woven blouses) and skirts that we came to recognize as the traditional dress of Maya women. The young men, dressed in jeans and shirts, could have blended in anywhere in the world, except that most of them were very short. At five foot one, I looked almost every one of them straight in the eye.

They each greeted us shyly, listening intently during the welcoming speeches. In spite of their earnest nodding, I wondered if they understood one word of what was being said. Then, after anxiously anticipating our turn to speak, we teachers stood to introduce ourselves: *What should I say? Remember to use simple words. Speak slowly.* We all glanced around furtively, trying to act like we weren't staring. *Who will be my student?* I'm certain they were wondering, *Who is my teacher?*

Assignments given, notebooks and Spanish-English dictionaries clutched close, each student-teacher pair went off to find a place to talk. A wrought-iron table in the courtyard became my classroom for the next two weeks.

What made me think I could do this? I don't know anything about how to teach a language, I thought, as I took out the photo album I'd brought, and we each cracked open our dictionary.

Remember they're more nervous than you are. You don't have to be perfect. Remember to have fun. Turns out that being able to laugh at yourself may be the single most important skill for a neophyte teacher.

The next morning the students introduced themselves in English in front of a group of thirty people. Spanish is their second language; one of the twenty-two Maya languages spoken in Guatemala is their native tongue.

The introductions followed a kind of formula, just like those dialogues in high school forty years ago.

Hello, my name is_____.

I am____years old.

I come from_____.

My family is made up of_____ .

One by one, the students came to the front of the room, stood, earnest and sweating—one young man gripping his hands behind his back to hide his tremors—and repeated the formula. Four short sentences each, then, "That's all!," sitting down to cheers and rousing applause.

A young man spoke last. I'd noticed him because of his radiant smile and raucous laugh. He stood now, hands sweeping back his shock of long black hair. He said the four sentences slowly, enunciating carefully: "I am Fernando, I am 25 years old." But before retreating to his chair, he added, "My father was killed when I was four months old. I am a survivor of the Guatemala civil war."

Guatemalan civil war? What is he talking about? What don't I know?

I had intended to travel to this third world country to teach, hoping to make some small contribution. But in those first days, I confronted a far different reality: that I had come to learn what I didn't know. I came to try to learn what it meant to be a survivor of the Guatemalan civil war.

Ten days later, after Fernando's introduction and the lunch with Balam, my plane home sat immobilized on the runway, shrouded in fog. To pass the time I figured I might as well meet my fellow passengers, so I turned to the teenage girl next to me who looked like she was from the States. Trying to make conversation I asked, "Were you visiting in Guatemala?"

No, she lives here with her family.

"Oh, where? I've been volunteering in Antigua, teaching English to Maya university students."

"We're American, but I've lived in Antigua my whole life. I go to a private high school here in Guatemala City."

She looked about the same age as my kids. "Are you applying to college in the States?" Yes, she was waiting to hear where she'd been accepted.

Full of Balam's story, and Fernando having described himself as a survivor, I asked, "So, what was it like living in Antigua during the civil war?"

She was well brought-up. Trying to be responsive to a middle-aged, gray-haired woman asking her a question, she paused, before turning to me politely, "What war?"

How could it happen that young people almost the same age, living close to one another, could have such radically different experiences of the same time? War had shattered Balam's and Fernando's lives. The same war had never touched the life of the young American girl. She had never even heard of it.

And why hadn't I known more about the civil war in Guatemala, a war that lasted for 36 years, the longest war in Latin America? How could something so horrific happen close to our borders, without me knowing more about it?

When I returned home, I set out to answer that question. A simple tally of articles comparing news coverage of El Salvador, Nicaragua and Guatemala between 1976 and 1996 revealed startling facts:

	El Salvador	Nicaragua	Guatemala
New York Times	829 articles	605 articles	322 articles
Washington Post	361 articles	242 articles	70 articles
Boston Globe	123 articles	54 articles	26 articles

But numbers tell just part of the story. In an article in the magazine *The Out Traveler*, author Gore Vidal puts it succinctly, "The truth doesn't get to us. The media exists to invent narratives and to disguise unpleasantries." (Gore Vidal, *The Out Traveler*, Summer 2007, page 30). Jean-Marie Simon, a photojournalist who covered Guatemala during the 1980s, offers a more in-depth explanation in her book, *Guatemala: Eternal Spring, Eternal Tyranny*.

> The US public maintains a provincial attitude about events outside its borders; what doesn't make the news must not be crucial, and this is often determined by some link to the United States...What little attention Guatemala did receive was, by 1980, even further diminished when foreign editors deemed that resources should next be directed toward El Salvador. While some journalists did cover Guatemala during the early 1980's, there was still little coverage at a time when government rural counterinsurgency was changing the country's landscape from one month to the next.

In *Stolen Continents*, author Ronald Wright echoes this:

> We hear little about this in the news. Too many journalists, priests, human rights investigators, and aid workers are among the dead. When reports do get out, the stories are so horrifying—Indian babies used as footballs, village elders herded into churches and burned alive—that decent, naive people find it difficult to believe them.

So that was why I knew so little about recent Guatemalan history. Now I set out to learn more.

. . . .

Three months later I returned to Guatemala for the first of several trips, trying to find answers to the question: "What war?" I met privately or in groups, with anyone who would talk to me, beginning with the students I had taught, and later, with their family members. I taped *testimonios* in English, in Spanish, sometimes in a mix of both, and in Kaqchikel, one of the Maya languages. People told their stories simply, sometimes crying, sometimes shrugging, sometimes making jokes to describe the most tragic situations. Often all three were interwoven in one interview, even sometimes in a single sentence.

Although these testimonios are recollections of events that happened many years before when the speakers were young children, each story had an immediacy, as if it had happened just the day before. In fact, often a speaker would begin by remembering the past: "Twenty years ago, my mother was killed by the soldiers…" and then continue in the present tense, "My brother steps in front of the soldiers begging them to take him and let our mother go."

When I first heard these testimonios I did not fully understand what was being said. But what I did understand is the way they were told—with urgency, with the unspoken plea: *Please believe this. It happened to me. I haven't been able to tell anyone. Please tell other people.*

In the newsletter *The Just Word*, Marcie Mersky, a North American who has lived in Guatemala for many years, describes collecting testimonies for the Commission for Historical Clarification, the Guatemalan Truth Commission (hereinafter referred to as the *CEH Report*):

> We needed to create a model that would salvage
> the elements that are lost when we focus simply on
> the documentation of human rights violations--a
> model that would better respect the testimony as a
> whole, and thus the integrity of the experience…It

should respect the logic and the voice of whoever
is doing the telling.

It wasn't until the testimonios had been translated, after I re-
flected on them, trying to make meaning out of what I had heard,
that various themes emerged. These are not superimposed, artificial
categories, but rather recurrent patterns that are embedded in the
stories themselves. The testimonios are presented together, according to these themes: the necessity of "breaking silence," telling the
truth even at great personal cost; the importance of reclaiming history; the suffering caused by displacement; the pervasiveness of fear;
the yearning for home. Although the testimonios are grouped, their
boundaries are permeable: while Hélida talks about the struggle to
maintain Maya identity, she also talks about the need to speak out,
and about fear. Robin speaks of the chaos, the violent unraveling of
social ties, and also about confronting racism. Balam and Mateo describe the fluid line between being Maya and "acting Ladino"[1] (a
term used in Guatemala synonymously with the term "mestizo" in
other Latin American countries).

And every single person, including Flor, who encouraged her
friends—*animaté!*—talked about being afraid: "After everything returned to being calm and normal, a huge fear stayed with us always,
that one day, the same thing would happen again."

I heard many personal experiences of terror, of being silenced
and of devastating loss, giving a human voice to what experts report

---

1. Refers both to descendants of the Spaniards and to people who are either born of mixed parentage and/or have chosen to assimilate to the dominant cultural group...scholars and human rights activists alike affirm the
importance of not underestimating the profound impact of racism on life
within Guatemala (Bastos and Camus 1996, Fischer and Brown 1996, War-
ren 1999) as quoted in "Telling Stories—Rethreading Lives: Among Maya
Ixil Women," Ins. J. *Leadership in Education*, 1999, Vol 2, No. 3, 207-227.

as the aftermath of trauma. This was to be expected. In *Trauma and Its Wake*, author R. Jancoff states: "Traumatic events destroy the victim's fundamental assumptions about the safety of the world, the positive value of the self, and the meaningful order of creation."

But there were other stories that were embedded in the testimonios: expressions of resistance, of resilience, even hope. In *Resilient Adults*, Gina Higgins defines resilient people as those who "do more than merely get through difficult emotional experiences, hanging on to inner equilibrium by a thread…[resilience is the] active process of self-righting and growth…" Self-righting and commitment to the future infuse these stories. In Guatemala, survivors of genocide are creating a new life for themselves, for their children, for their country.

In their article "Testimony as Ritual and Evidence in Psychotherapy for Political Refugees," Inger Agger and Soren Jensen state that telling the trauma story is a "healing ritual, as well as a condemnation of injustice":

> The trauma story becomes a testimony…(that) has both a private dimension, which is confessional and spiritual, and a public aspect, which is political and judicial. The use of the word testimony links both meanings, giving a new and larger dimension to the patient's individual experience.

It became evident that telling their stories helped the individuals who gave testimonios to see their experiences in a broader, more political context. Evident because they said so.

I have made every effort to respect the "logic and voice of whoever did the telling." I have not altered the words used to recount these truths. This book, then, is the story of what I heard.

2

The War in Context

> "I don't want to live in my past, but I want my past to live in me. Memory is the soul of history."
>
> —Elie Wiesel

TO UNDERSTAND THE DEVASTATING CIVIL WAR, referred to in Guatemala as *la violencia* or the "internal armed conflict," it is necessary to go back to the invasion by Spanish conquistadors in 1521. The Spanish colonization of Central America was driven by the quest for gold and by the desire to "save souls" by converting the "heathen" to Catholicism. The lives of the Maya and other, smaller indigenous groups in what would become modern Guatemala, were irrevocably transformed by the Spanish conquest. Since that time, the history of the indigenous people of Guatemala has been marked by subjugation, colonialization and foreign intervention. These events, although occurring almost 500 years ago, are still referred to as "the conquest," clear evidence of the effect that this history continues to have on present-day Guatemala.

As in other countries in Latin America, Guatemalan civil institutions have been fragile and unstable. What distinguishes Guatemala, however, is the length of time and the extent to which the military has remained so deeply entrenched in power since independence from Spain in 1821. And, in fact, independence from

Spain did little to liberate the indigenous people, as Ronald Wright observes in *Stolen Continents:* "It soon became clear that independence from the Spanish Empire did not mean independence for the Maya. For them…the so-called liberation was merely a white settler takeover…"

The notable exception to this military domination was the ten years from 1944–1954, called the "Decade of Spring." The governments of Juan José Arévalo (1944–1951) and Jacobo Arbenz (1951–1954) were democatically elected. Arévalo referred to his government as "spiritual socialism," declaring, "We are socialists because we live in the 20th century." Later, the Arbenz government attempted significant land reforms that challenged business interests of the United States, particularly those of the United Fruit Company. In response, United Fruit exerted political influence on the Eisenhower administration, resulting in the 1954 CIA-backed invasion which overthrew Arbenz, and installed a puppet government.

What followed was a half century of U.S. involvement in the internal affairs of Guatemala, during which right-wing military governments were supported. Military dictators Lucas García (1978–1982) and Efraín Ríos Montt (1982–1983) were trained in contra-insurgency warfare and torture techniques at the School of the Americas in Fort Benning, Georgia. Under their jurisdiction state-sponsored terror became a reality, and the "scorched earth" (*la tierra arrasada*) policy was implemented in the highlands against rural Maya villages. The Official Report of the Human Rights Office of the Archdiocese of Guatemala, (hereinafter referred to as the *REHMI Report* for its Spanish acronym) describes this as…"a grisly holocaust for people living in the so-called conflictive areas."(*REHMI*,Volume 3, page 112). I first heard la tierra arrasada mentioned by Fernando who described this policy: "In the 1980s, during the rule of General Efraín Ríos Montt, brutal practices were used against the *guerrilleros*, anyone they thought were communists or who they thought were supporting them. La tierra arrasada was the practice, that is burning the land, killing everyone in the villages who the army suspected of having anything to do with the guerrillas."

In June 1994, Guatemala's Truth Commission was established. The three members of the Commission were charged with the task of clarifying "with objectivity, equity, and impartiality, the human rights violations and acts of violence connected with the armed confrontation that caused suffering among the Guatemalan people." (Prologue, *CEH Report*). The Truth Commission was mandated to "issue a report...containing the results of its investigations and its recommendations for national reconciliation and promotion of a culture of tolerance...The report would not individualize responsibilities for specific human rights violations or have judicial objectives or consequences."[2]

On December 29, 1996, peace accords were signed ending 36 years of civil war. In 1997, the Truth Commission began taking testimonies from over 9,000 war victims. And on April 24, 1998, Bishop Juan Gerardi presented the final report of The Human Rights Office of the Archdiocese of Guatemala, *Guatemala, Nunca más!* Two days later, Bishop Gerardi was brutally murdered outside his residence in Guatemala City.

In February, 1999, an audience of more than 10,000 people gathered to hear the Truth Commission present its report, which revealed these staggering facts:

"During the internal armed confrontation there were 626 massacres, 1.5 million people were displaced, 150,000 became refugees, and more than 200,000 were dead or disappeared. In the Ixil region alone between 70% and 90% of the villages were burned to the ground. [These were]...acts committed with the intent to destroy in whole or in part, numerous groups of Mayans. [They] were not isolated acts or excesses committed by soldiers who were out of control, nor were they the result of possible improvisation by midlevel Army command. With great consternation, the Commission concludes that many massacres and other human rights violations committed against these groups obeyed a higher, strategically planned policy...."

The *CEH Report* documented that "State forces and related paramilitary groups were responsible for 93% of the violations" (page 20) and that "83% of the victims were Mayans". The Report stated, unequivocally, that the army had conducted acts of genocide against the Maya people, acts committed "with the intent to destroy, in whole or in part, groups identified by their common ethnicity."

In the chapter entitled "Peace and Reconciliation," the *CEH Report* "dedicates its work to the memory of the dead and other victims of over three decades of fratricidal violence in Guatemala" concluding that:

> To achieve true reconciliation and construct a new democratic and participatory nation which values its multiethnic and pluricultural nature, the whole of society must...assume the commitments of the peace process. This...requires a profound and complex effort, which Guatemalan society owes to the thousands of brave men and women who sought to obtain full respect for human rights and the democratic rule of law and so laid the foundation for this new nation. Among these, Monsignor Juan Gerardi Conedera remains at the forefront.

If memory is the soul of history, as Elie Wiesel declares, then all Guatemalans must be allowed, in fact encouraged, to speak out about the past in order to "construct a new democratic and participatory nation," a new Guatemala.

3

The Elemental Right to Remember and to Speak

> "Memory has a clear preventive function. Preventing a recurrence of tragedy is largely dependent on dismantling the structures that made such horror possible."
>
> —*REHMI Report*

> "It was necessary to enable victims to speak about their experiences—to restore the elemental right to remember, a right that was systemically denied through the imposition of terror."
>
> —*Marcie Mersky in* The Just Word

IN MARCH 2005, THREE MONTHS AFTER MY INITIAL TRIP, one of the other teachers and I returned to Guatemala City hoping to interview some of our former students. All of them had been invited to attend a meeting to share their experiences of the civil war, but I had no idea whether any of them would actually come, or if they did, whether they would be willing to tell their stories.

Nine students showed up. I had made arrangements to have an interpreter, so I would not have to depend on my limited Spanish. To begin, I explained that I was trying to learn about their personal experiences, that they could either respond to specific questions or tell their story in any way they wanted to. I assured them that I would understand what they said because their words would be translated, and I promised that I would not write anything without their permission. Then I turned on the tape recorder and waited for someone to begin.

During the long silence I remembered what psychiatrist Judith Herman said in *Trauma and Recovery*: "The ordinary response to atrocities is to banish them from consciousness. Certain violations of the social compact are too terrible to utter aloud: this is the meaning of the word unspeakable." Would anyone be able to speak?

We all waited, silently. Then Fernando, the young man whose simple introduction had started me on this journey, reached for the tape recorder and began talking. After several minutes, I gestured for him to stop, and the interpreter turned to me, speaking English. Just as I was fully grasping what Fernando had said, my colleague touched my shoulder, and whispered, "Don't have her translate. It's interrupting him—the memories, the flow—you need to just let him talk."

What, no translation? I shook my head. *No, no, I need the translation. How will I understand what he's saying?*

Fernando sat, waiting.

Throughout my whole life, I have been in love with words: parsing, interpreting, questioning. But now I wouldn't be able to fully understand the words I was hearing. I had to just sit there, listening. Absorbing, without interrupting. No probing questions. No interpreting. I had to comprehend in the most elemental way, witnessing with my eyes and heart.

· · · · · · ·

"I don't want to forget. Now more than ever, I want to have with me all that happened in the war, and I want to tell about it...If not, the memory is lost."

—Fernando

FERNANDO'S WAR

Fernando is a 25-year-old K'iche' Maya man studying law at the University of San Carlos. He is the youngest of 11 children. His family were *campesinos* (peasant farmers) in the Altiplano (highlands).

I was born on June 30, 1980. I was four months old when my father was killed by the soldiers...and, *bueno* (okay), my mother told me the truth about what happened. That we were persecuted by the army, we had to flee, and that we must not tell the truth to anybody, because our lives were in danger. We always had to invent a different history to tell people, because my mother told us that it was very dangerous to tell the truth to other people here in Guatemala City...My father Reyes and my older brother Daniel were murdered by the soldiers in 1980 in our village, Macalajau, Uspantán, which is in the Quiché Department in the north of

Fernando

Guatemala. Another of my brothers, Demetrio, was kidnapped [at that time]. My older sister, Bernadina, was kidnapped in 1983 here in Guatemala City. We have still not found her; she is still disappeared.

I want to say to you that for me, the war has affected me more than anything else in my life…we have problems, psychological problems. Ooooh, and the hardest part about the war is that we lost the process of our lives, we lost our childhood, many things that will never be able to be repeated.

My family, yes, had a direct participation in the war. My father supported the guerrillas, he was a person who was convinced that in our country things needed to be changed because the indigenous people are very poor and it's very difficult to improve their situation. Life in the communities was very hard and my father thought it was necessary to fight, and so he was killed by the soldiers.

But my mother always told us the truth, we always knew the truth about what had happened. I think the most difficult was that we always had to lie, and we had to change our names, all of my family had different names. My brother, my sister, my father, my uncles, had been assassinated in my community, then in 1983 my sister was kidnapped, so we were still being pursued by the military. We had to change houses many times here in Guatemala City, and afterwards all of my siblings were put into schools in different places. I have family that escaped to Mexico, and family that fled to Spain, where they still live even after the war.

But, those of us who are students, we can still have a happy ending. We have the opportunity to study in the university. So, I think that this is what we have to value, we have to be thankful that we have this opportunity. We're lucky to have this different story. But it's not the common story, because other families are still living in poverty. Sometimes, when I look at the shoe-shiners, when I look at the people that are prostitutes, or all those people who are working as domestic servants, they have a situation different from ours.

That is, we are lucky in this sense, but I think that we haven't been able to overcome everything that has happened. We are still suffering from racism, discrimination, exclusion, and we still live in a very divided society. Well, what I believe is that, well…for me, anyway, what most affects me…well….

Fernando cried. His friends sat, staring away into their own distance, then, one by one they got up to touch his shoulder, bring him a paper cup of water, or walk out of the room. No one said a word.

What I believe is that we've lost a lot in the war. I mean, my father had an ideology, my mother, all my family, they actively participated in the changes of the country. I've already lost a lot of family, and we lost so much, and I don't want the war to keep affecting me anymore, I want to overcome all these things, because I believe that until we are stronger ourselves, it will be difficult to support others.

There are a lot of people who are still affected, and they have to heal their wounds. We have to strengthen ourselves, as victims of the war, as survivors, because in the end, this is what we are. We are survivors. And although we are survivors, this doesn't mean that they haven't destroyed our lives. We lost the most important thing we had, our family relationships, right? We lost a way of life, of our existence, that we will never be able to get back. Never.

The feeling of surviving came from my mother who protected us. Along the way, we met many good people who helped us. Even though our future was already marked…my mother couldn't speak Spanish, we were in such a big city, a racist city, and with eight kids, well, surely we would have had a different future than the one that we have now. However, we managed to defy destiny, and we're alive.

If they ask me if I am resentful, no, I don't think I'm resentful, but I think that these things hurt, and with much difficulty we will forget them, too. Yes, the pain and suffering lasted a long time, but I think that we can transfer all of this, or at least, what I have done with all the pain that I have, I have converted it into energy, that day-by-day allows me to continue. But during all of these problems I had many crises, emotional, psychological—very strong—and I have had to go into treatment to be able to go on. Because, yes, sometimes, you don't see the light at the end of the tunnel.

Fernando's voice caught, he sobbed, so quietly you could barely hear him. But he couldn't go on. Someone handed him a Kleenex.

In the work that I have done, especially the cases of exhumations, I can see that some people are still very affected, when they are searching for their disappeared family members. I am aware that I'm not prepared to support other people, because I am also still very affected. I haven't overcome this, and I don't want to forget. Now more than ever, I want to have with me all that happened in the war, and I want to tell about it, because the war affected my mother a lot, and my brothers and sisters, and everyone who had to hide their history, and who had to invent histories, who had to change the truth so that nothing more would happen to them.

When I first went to school I wanted to study journalism, but instead I studied law, because I became aware that many human rights abuses were committed against us, simply because we were indigenous. I believe that our profession can help us a lot, and that as a lawyer I can contribute to the changes in my country, and work to avoid the abuse against the Maya, that still persists to this day.

Right up until this present moment, we have had to fight a lot and suffer through all of this, to be able to get back our rights. I think all children should know the truth of what happened, they have to know the history of their country. If not, the memory is lost. In the case of my nieces and nephews—yes, at least I have nieces and nephews—I think they should know where they come from, who their grandfather was, who their aunts and uncles were.

They may live in a different situation now, but they should know the truth, because this is the only way they are going to truly understand, and be able to take a coherent point of view in discussions, and be people who really give a damn. And, moreover, they should fight against all the horrible acts committed in the war, so that they don't ever happen again. For a long time we were afraid, we were afraid because of what had happened to us, and of what was going to happen to us. We thought of forgetting what had happened to us, but more than ever I think that we should not forget. All of the people of the world must know what has occurred here in Guatemala.

There was a heaviness to the silence when Fernando finished. As though we were collectively holding our breath. There were twelve of us around the table, but each person seemed to be alone in their own world; no one was looking at anyone else. I waited, speechless, because although I had not understood the exact meaning of every word of Fernando's story, I had fully absorbed the feelings. And it was obvious that everyone else had both understood and absorbed everything. Perhaps what he had just done was dangerous; perhaps no one else could take the same risk. There was enormous social and political pressure to forget, to go forward, to live in the present. Maybe Fernando was unique in his need to tell his story.

In her book *Trama and Recovery*, author Judith Herman describes the terror that many survivors experience when they are "breaking silence" this way:

> In order to escape accountability for his crimes, the
> perpetrator does everything in his power to pro-
> mote forgetting. Secrecy and silence are the per-
> petrator's first line of defense.

I wondered if this terror extended to hearing another survivor's
story; did it drag the listeners back into their own traumatic pasts, re-
traumatizing them? Would anyone else dare to speak?

And then, Víctor reached for the microphone and started to talk.
His memories began with his mother running back to the house to
get blankets to keep the family warm when they hid in the mountains. He never saw her again.

. . . .

> "We stayed between two fires, between the guer-
> rillas and the soldiers."
> —Víctor

VÍCTOR'S WAR

Víctor is a 26-year-old Mam Maya man in his fifth year studying political science and international relations at Universidad Rafael
Landívar. He paused often as he told his story. When I got to know
him better, I realized that he'd been carefully searching for the right
words, trying to be respectful, trying to avoid expressing his anti-
American feelings.

Ahh, I didn't think I was going to be next, but okay, my turn
would come anyway. I was four years old when they came to
burn the houses in the village and assassinate the people. And my
mom, she thought it would be possible to protect me and my
brother. We're the youngest in the family, we were at home with
her...so she took us out of the house and left us at a coffee field,
and she went back to the house to get the money and the things
that she'd need to cover us, to keep us warm, that we would

need on the mountain. So she went back, but she didn't make it to the house, because she was blown up by the army. She was killed in that moment.

And me and my brother were abandoned where she left us, so the neighbors that went by picked us up and took us with them. My older brothers were working in the fields with my fa-

Victor

ther, so they weren't with us. Three or four days later we were reunited with my father, and since I was the youngest, I was crying and I wanted to find my mom, but my father told me that I wasn't ever going to see her again, because she'd been assassinated.

The village where I'm from, Centro Uno, is one of the first villages that Father Guillermo Woods founded in the Ixcán. He was working for land reform because the government hadn't given land to the peasants, so at least that way we had some land to grow crops. He was a Texan from the United States, which means that not all *gringos* are bad people.

Like you, you are now with us.

[Back then], my mother, that is all my relatives, don't know what communism is, what capitalism is, don't know anything about the situation. We were caught between two fires, between the guerrillas and the soldiers. Because the guerrillas were not well-informed either of what the fight was about. All my relatives, they're innocent people!

I think that left a mark on my life that led me to study political science. One time General Alejandro Gramajo, who was a minister in the government of Vinicio Cerezo gave a lecture at the university about a book he had written, and he said many false things. But nobody else spoke up, they just listened and accepted what he said, justifying himself by saying that 'all wars are dirty'…I decided I couldn't miss this opportunity to say something to this man, like, why didn't they prevent the war, and, him being one of the main actors, why didn't he do something?

So, this is what I can tell you about the violence; it has influenced the fact that we are a society with our heads bowed down, one in which we cannot say things directly because we are afraid. In other countries, in Europe, in the U.S., the people express their opinions without fear, but it's different here. People just stay in their community, and do nothing.

But I believe in keeping the history alive. I believe that we must confront the authoritarianism of the State, to confront what they did. We must look for a solution.

After that each person took a turn, speaking extemporaneously, without notes, following the thread of their past. Each testimonio was brief, like a poem, capturing the essence of memory. Later, I read a poem by the African-American poet Lucille Clifton, that could have served as the introduction to María's memories, those of a little girl who could only tell her pillow her deepest terror.

shapeshifter poem # 4

the poem at the end of the world
is the poem the little girl breathes
into her pillow   the one
she cannot tell   the one
there is no one to hear   this poem
is a political poem   is a war poem   is a
universal poem but it is not about
these things   this poem
is about one human heart   this poem
is the poem at the end of the world

· · · · · · ·

> "I had an experience that left an impression on me,
> and left me with many fears. I don't know why I
> didn't tell my parents. Maybe I was afraid."
>   —María

MARÍA'S WAR

María is a 25-year-old K'iche' Maya woman studying architecture at the University of San Carlos. She arrived early for class
every morning impeccably dressed in the *traje* (traditional dress) of
her original community in the Quiché.

I was born in Quiché in 1980, at the worst time during the
civil war, and I didn't understand a lot of what was happening,
but I noticed certain things. Many people on my mom's side of
the family belonged to the guerrillas. They had two options, either to die or join the guerrillas. So they decided to join, and
many of them disappeared. Some were killed, others were ex-
iled in Mexico, and others came to the capital. My family left
their town, and went to Santa Cruz del Quiché with my grandparents. I was about five or six and I didn't understand everything that happened until many years later.

But I had an experience that left an impression on me, and
left me with many fears. I don't know why I didn't tell my parents. Maybe because I was afraid. We lived in a place with a lot
of *milpa* (cornfields), the houses were far apart, and one day
when I was coming back from the store, I saw about four soldiers pointing a gun at a woman who had her baby on her back,
about four months old. They were asking her where her husband was, and she didn't want to tell them, so they were push-
ing her from one to the other and they were hurting her. I don't
know what she told them, but they threw her to the ground

and shot her from behind, killing the baby and her. That was a horrible experience for me, because I was just a little girl and my character was just being formed.

And things like this happened every day since our house was on a main road and the military were constantly going by. And for a while we could hear a lot of gunshots being fired. I was very frightened, but I didn't tell my mother until I was about eleven.

My family helped the guerrillas, and I think that was a good deed, because there were many people suffering, many people in the resistance, and that was a way to help them. For instance, one of my uncles kept food at the house. At night, many sacks of food, sugar, coffee, corn were left at the house. He would take it in and out again in the morning, and this went on over and over again. All of that food went to the guerrillas' campsites. Of course, the army didn't know about it, or we would all have been killed.

That's the hardest experience that my family lived, except what happened to some of the others who were directly involved with the guerrillas, and they didn't come back until the peace was signed in 1996. They didn't know what was happening to their families, whether they were alive or dead, until '96 when they came back. That's what I have to say.

. . . .

"The state is the one that killed…the civilians did not know anything, but then the army would come.'
—Elías

ELÍAS'S WAR

Elías approached me several times, asking shyly when he could give his testimonio. He listened intently, tears streaming down his cheeks, as other survivors told their memories; when it was his turn to speak, his voice and hands quivered. He was ten and eleven during the worst years of the war. Elías is a 33-year-old K'iche' Maya man studying law at the University of San Carlos.

One day, my brother and I went to school and when we got out at 12:30, we started walking towards my grandparents' house. We heard sounds like fireworks at Christmas time, but it was machine guns and the bullets were hitting the straw roofs of the houses. My grandparents told us "Stay here, don't go home, because who knows what's going on!" They put us in the kitchen, you could hear the bullets, and the soldiers shouting, "Give it more fire! Higher, higher!" My uncle told us to get under the table, so that the things that were falling from the roof wouldn't hurt us.

My grandfather closed the door because we were afraid. Then a soldier pushed open the door and said, "Where are the guerrillas?" My grandfather said, "Here there are no guerrillas. We are the only ones here, it's just that we're afraid, that's why we're hiding." And then my grandfather and uncle told the soldier, "We're going to get our papers, don't worry, we're not guerrillas." And they went to get their IDs and papers, and when they came back there was a different soldier behind the door, and he didn't see that my grandfather and uncle had their papers, and he shot them. Yes, they died there.

The next day there was an article in the paper, 'Two Guerrilla Chiefs Were Killed' it said. But, no, my grandfather was dedicated to the Catholic religion, he taught religious classes. But the headline in *El Gráfico*, that was the newspaper, had that headline, "Two Guerilla Chiefs Were Killed."

Many people spoke briefly, though there was no time limit imposed. Flory, however, talked for over an hour, her words like a powerful stream that had broken through a dam and could not be stopped.

....

"They put us children under a table covered with plastic sheets with the women on the other side. Then the men. In the farthest corner were the children. It was to protect the youngest generation."
—Flory

FLORY'S WAR

Flory has a psychology degree from the University of San Carlos and works as a counselor with women victims of the violence. She is a 33-year-old Poqomchi' Maya woman.

When I was ten years old, that was when the war began for me. I barely studied fourth grade. The school year started, but there wasn't a day when they didn't take us out of the school or put us all in a single room, about 500 or 600 children in just one place, all crammed in there. It was frightening, because many soldiers came often to the school. One day they stuck some of us in the bathroom, they closed us in there, and in front of me they abused several of the girls. It was very difficult because they grabbed a friend, they grabbed her legs and threw her down. The soldiers forced her legs opened, and jumped on top of her. We didn't understand. I went home and told my mother, and she said, "No more school!"

We dug tunnels between our house and our neighbors, and we kept in contact with them so that if the soldiers came to someone's house, the others would come to help. We had codes to communicate with each other. For example, if the soldiers came to my house, we would pull the string connecting us all, to say "Open the door!" They immediately would open all of the tunnels until we got to the last house, and there was a hole where all of us children and women stayed. The men gathered a little further out. We hid like this many, many times.

We felt that the nights were so long. I remember that passage as dark, very dark, like there wasn't any light. In fact, there wasn't any electricity, we just used candles. What I remember is the dark. I see it as a tunnel without an exit. Without any exit at all.

The young people (today) did not live this, but in some way they are still victims of the violence. I hope that one day this changes with the future generations. Without a doubt there are testimonies that can help them understand. It is necessary to confront these things that are pulling us down, to clean all of this up. We must make it transparent, and leave it behind in order to move forward.

In these testimonios given by Fernando, Víctor, María, Elías and Flory, we can already see themes emerging: the importance of speaking the truth for individual healing, for reclaiming community identity and dignity, and for preventing future violence.

Fernando's mother told her children the truth, but told them not to tell anyone else. They were forced to lie, which included changing their traditional dress and taking false identities, in an attempt to protect themselves. Now, he says, "I want to have with me all that happened in the war, and I want to tell about it": telling the truth, not forgetting, is of vital importance to reclaiming his sense of self, and his Maya identity.

Víctor describes how the violence and fear have silenced the victims, that "we are a society with our heads bowed down" where people are afraid to state their opinions.

And each person emphasized the importance of telling the truth to the next generation in order to prevent the violence from occurring again, echoing the name of the *REHMI Report, Guatemala, Nunca más! (Never Again!)*

> The memory of atrocities…is an important aspect of violence prevention…Without public acknowledgment and social censure of the guilty, the perpetrators may ultimately be strengthened in their positions.

4

Reclaiming History

> "...a society that forgets, whose
> collective memory has blurred
> over, is subject to all kinds of
> ghosts."
>
> —María López Vigil

IT WASN'T ONLY YOUNG AMERICANS living in Guatemala like the girl I met on the plane, who didn't know about the violence destroying a people and their culture. Many Guatemalans, both Ladino and Maya themselves, did not know what was happening in other communities, either because of poor communication, or because the culture of silence made sharing information a potentially dangerous act.

Since 1996 when the peace accords were signed, there have been frequent and insistent calls for the government and the military to disclose and acknowledge their roles and responsibility for the devastation perpetuated against the indigenous population.

The *REHMI Report* states:

> The government should publicly acknowledge the
> facts and its responsibility in the massive, system-
> atic violation of the human rights of the
> Guatemalan people...They should acknowledge
> that this happened, that it was unjust, and that they

43

are committed to taking the necessary measures to avoid any recurrence. This official acknowledgment must be included in informational and educational programs to ensure that it reaches all sectors of Guatemalan society, particularly those most affected by the war. The government must avoid measures that contradict this overall position. Such measures would include decorating or honoring human rights violators, including former presidents responsible for State terrorism.

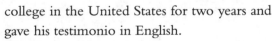

"The people didn't know what was really going on, I am including myself. I only learned this a long time later from what was reported in the newspapers, even though not everything that was happening was told there."

—Porfirio

PORFIRIO'S WAR

Porfirio was my driver during a trip to the Altiplano. He described the culture of silence and the effort it took for him to learn and reclaim history. He is a 31-year-old Maya Kaqchikel man who works as an agronomy consultant with *campesinos*. He had gone to

college in the United States for two years and gave his *testimonio* in English.

In Santa María where I live, we didn't hear about all this, and some people even today don't know if there was war or not. Perhaps recently they have heard that there was fighting between guerillas and the army, but really what happened they have never found out. In 1992

Porfirio

there was a massacre in El Aguacate of San Andrés Itzapa, because they showed it on the TV news, but not too many people from our village saw it because not everyone had a television.

But it was always said that there were guerrillas and the army, but really what was going on the people didn't know, I am including myself. I only learned this a long time later from what was reported in the newspapers, even though not everything that was happening was told there. I became more aware of all of this where I was studying (later) because there they did tell what was really happening and it wasn't until then that I became more interested in what was going on in Guatemala.

What I did know about was what they called 'forced recruitment.' The military made two attempts to take me away, but I was only 13 years old. My father came and talked to them so that they wouldn't take me, but, yes, at that time in Santa María and Santiago, the two towns were competing for who had the most young men in the army. In fact, Santiago is the one that has more men, they even didn't have to recruit them, they just showed up on their own because they had that much desire to belong to the Guatemalan army. But they didn't really know what they were headed to. It wasn't until they were already in the army that they realized what the reality was. Much later they repented having joined up, but they couldn't get out at that time. Because if you left they killed you, they searched for you, and they killed you because you were a defector from the army.

One of the things that went on in Santa María were the civilian self-defense patrols. But really they didn't do anything, they just presented themselves on Sunday, they marched all day, they were trained in all kinds of combat, and then they made rounds of the town at night. There were two shifts, they started from 6:00 to midnight, and then another group came at midnight until 6:00 in the morning. The army came once a month and stayed for a week. Seeing all this, the people did not know what was happening, as I have told you, and let me say again, many people from my village really did not know what happened in Guatemala.

I myself did not have the experience of something like a family member who disappeared, but you heard about these things and dead bodies appeared on the outskirts of the village. Three or four tied up or thrown in the tall grasses, but they were not people from our village, they were people from other places. And the violence and the bodies that appeared at that time were people who had been kidnapped, or people that they said belonged to the guerrillas, this is what you heard, and later no one said anything.

The most I ever heard directly about the violence was from a guy I'd gone to school with. He joined the army and became a Kaibil, one of the special commando forces, you know, they're the ones who wear maroon berets? They have a patch on their uniform that's a blazing sword. A lot of the boys wanted to join because those uniforms are really nice, and they thought they'd look really handsome and the girls would like them. Also, I think they got paid a little more.

I ran into this guy in a bar in the City several years later. I almost didn't recognize him, his eyes were bloodshot, he was so drunk he was falling down. He grabbed hold of me, and started talking. He told me things he'd done, that are so terrible, so disgusting and degrading, I've never told anyone. You wouldn't believe the things he told me. He'd been a nice guy, a little wild, but still a good person, when we were in school. Now he was a crazy man. He said he'd done things that made him hate himself. He hated himself so much, all he wanted to do was drink.

No one in our town would talk to him. He was a young guy, too. Now it seemed like his life was over.

I believe that one of the objectives of the civil war was to exterminate the poor people, or exterminate the indigenous people, because the majority of those that were in the army were indigenous, and those that made up the guerrillas were also indigenous, and they were the ones killing each other. One of the objectives of the people in power in Guatemala was to finish off the indigenous people, so that they could remain in power, and maybe they partially achieved it. But the majority of the country is still indigenous; they are the people who are still struggling to survive and to get ahead. Guatemala is the only country in Central America that still has lots of indigenous people. So I think the people in power believe that the only way to maintain control is to keep repressing them, abusing them, in different ways that still exist in Guatemala.

I think that there are many consequences that are a result of the war, there are still problems that exist and this has made the country very unstable. In reality, I think that signing of the peace accords has not really changed much, because the same social problems that existed even before the war exploded still exist. Maybe what has changed is that now you don't hear of the guerillas, but the army is still in power. Here in Guatemala the military is who is in charge, not the government.

. . . .

The necessity of providing information and education about the government role in "systematic human rights violations" was emphasized in the *REHMI Report*. However, as late as 2001, many people, including Marcie Mersky, who worked as a field coordinator on the *REHMI* and *CEH Reports*, stated that "the history of the armed conflict and the consequences to date is not available in the school curriculum."

But perhaps this has changed since 2001. Perhaps now there was, as mandated by the *REHMI Report*, an "official acknowledgement...to ensure that it reaches all sectors of Guatemalan society, particularly those most affected by the war." To find out I reviewed several social studies textbooks to see how the civil war is presented. In *Aventuras 3: Medio Social*, a third grade social studies textbook, the discussion of the war focuses primarily on naming various guerrilla groups. There is also a photograph of a Maya family hiking in the mountains with the caption: "The armed conflict left thousands of families disintegrated and without a home. Many of them had to abandon their communities to save their lives." However, there no information regarding the role of the government in state-sponsered violence or the reality of the Maya genocide. Perhaps this omission results from a desire to include only information that is considered "age-appropriate". To determine if this was the case, I reviewed a textbook for 7th graders called *Estudios Sociales 7*. The following statement appears in it: "The internal armed conflict lasted many years, and all the Guatemalan population was involved in it. In one way or another all the families in the country were affected by the death, destruction, and pain suffered by the country." Although accurate, this statement remains vague and avoids assigning responsiblity to the government for human rights abuses.

In its conclusions the *CEH Report* states unequivocally that "agents of the State of Guatemala...committed acts of genocide against groups of Mayan people." In light of this reality, we must ask whether the true history of the civil war itself has been "disappeared."

. . . .

Whatever history is being taught in schools is clearly not the history that these Maya children lived. Elías supports Mersky's point in his own words:

You couldn't talk, because you never knew who you were talking with...I am happy that you collect these small testimonies and I hope that you can write articles or a book, because what we don't have in Guatemala is this: history. It's not written, it's only told occasionally, what we experienced, but mostly this is forgotten. Those of us who are older, we lived it, but the younger ones didn't, they don't know it. There's no history, there are no books.

Laura did not learn about la violencia from her parents: "Neither my father nor my mother told me the history, rather I have seen it." She describes how she came to learn the history of her own country once she began working as a K'iche'-Spanish interpreter with Sister Barbara Ford, a Sisters of Charity nun from New York. Sister Barbara had worked as a nurse and community activist in Guatemala for twenty years, and had assisted collecting testimonies for the *REHMI Report*. When Sister Barbara was murdered during a robbery in 2001, Laura was devastated. Since that time, she has recommitted herself to working as a community mental health worker collecting testimonios from victims of the violence. She said, "I feel that being in each community and listening to each person that tells me about what happened to them, I feel like I also have been inside of this history. I think that this is a mission that I have. I must speak for them, because they are not here...Now, by sharing their history, I am a voice for them."

She contrasts the realities of what she has heard in the communities to what she had been taught:

"In school, the history that we study is about Christopher Columbus, or other histories that happened in nearby countries, but a real history of our community or of our country we never learned in school...Even though I didn't know anything about the history, in my work I learned what really happened. There are many versions, because some say: 'It's because of the army,' others say, 'It's because of the guerrillas.' What that helps me to understand is that, despite the fact that the people lived the conflict directly, they don't know the root of the conflict. So many parents don't know how to tell the history because if there is no root, then you don't know how to begin to tell it. Then there are many young people who don't know the history."

What is the consequence for a community, for a nation, when people do not know their history? No one taught Porfirio, Elías or Laura the true history of their country. There was no national narrative, no agreed-upon and accepted version of historical events. Rather they pieced together the past from various sources: "A guy in a bar told me…"; "I heard a rumor that…"; "You never knew who you were talking to…" They had to gather information themselves to try to create a coherent story of what had happened. Today they are committed to making sure that the younger generation learns the truth—an accurate version of the past—which has everything to do with the present and the future of Guatemala.

5
Maintaining Integrity

"The massacres, scorched earth operations, forced disappearances and executions of Mayan authorities, leaders and spiritual guides, were not only an attempt to destroy the social base of the guerillas, but above all, to destroy the cultural values that ensured cohesion and collective action in Mayan communities."

—*CEH Report*

ANTHROPOLOGISTS AND SOCIOLOGISTS STUDY THE FORMATION and transmission of culture, as well as the effect of cultural change and disintegration on a people. In this chapter we hear first-hand accounts from individuals who have endured attempts to destroy their culture. Here they speak of their resistance and efforts to preserve their Maya identity.

. . . .

"It takes a lot of strength and awareness to be in the middle of this racist world, because if we're not aware, we can't hold up, and our identity will be lost."

—Hélida

HÉLIDA'S WAR

Hélida is a 28-year-old Kaqchikel Maya woman. She has just graduated with a law degree from the University of San Carlos, and is working with indigenous women. She recently began studying with a Maya shaman to learn about indigenous spirituality. In this testimonio, Hélida talks about living in a racist culture and her efforts to resist deculturalization.

I am twenty-eight years old. My family emigrated from a village to Mixco which is right at the edge of Guatemala City. My whole family has been discriminated against because everyone else there are Ladinos. And my family is indigenous.

I was little during the war. I remember hearing the helicopters that flew over the town, and my grandparents would tell me that I should hide. I asked them what would happen, and they told me that they were looking for someone, for the guerrillas. I always grew up with this fear—when I hear the helicopters I remember that someone is being hunted down. When I was about ten years old, I asked a lot of questions about why photos appeared on the walls of the markets. My mother told me that I should never say anything, because something could happen to me or to the family.

This is the only thing that happened to me and my family during the war…we lost our customs, and the life in our village. It has been difficult for my family—maintaining our integrity, our indigenous culture, in the middle of a Ladino village. No one in my family was injured that I know of, so I haven't lived with that pain, but I have shared much of the pain of my friends that are from the Ixcán region. They have made this a reality for me, and thanks to this, I decided to read more about the histories of the massacres, and everything that happened in the internal armed conflict. Because if I hadn't, I wouldn't be aware of all this, of the reality of Guatemalan history.

Because no one talks about this in the City. The person who has lived it is the only one that knows it, and he can't talk about it because it's dangerous. The problem is that there is always intimidation. I've had experiences with my law school classmates when I tried to talk about human rights violations. They told me that it would get us into trouble, because we don't really know who's against it! No one would do it with me because they said they were afraid. They said, 'Oh, you have a great conscience, but you don't know who will be the ones that might hurt you or something could happen, that could be a result of the internal armed conflict.'

I think that the war is one of the elements that forms the basis of the discrimination and the racism that still exists in Guatemala. We are still discriminated against, and even though one may achieve a certain level of education or become a professional, the limits of discrimination are always there. It takes a lot of strength and awareness to be in the middle of this racist world, because if we're not aware, we can't hold up, and our identity will be lost.

And I think that for me, now, this is my fight: to maintain a personal identity, and try to promote it with the people I interact with. And I think it is a very difficult job.

While Hélida talks about the subtle and damaging effect of trying to survive in a society where racial discrimination is a fact of life, Mateo focuses more on the officially sanctioned programs designed to eradicate indigenous culture.

. . . .

"Rios Montt killed the population because he believed Maya people were to blame for the country's underdevelopment and that by eliminating
them, Guatemala would prosper."
—Mateo

MATEO'S WAR

Mateo is a 30-year-old Q'anjobal Maya man who graduated
from the university with an agronomy degree. He works as a Spanish teacher.

Really (the main cause of the violence) is simply racism or discrimination towards the Maya language speakers. For example,
Miguel Angel Asturias, who won the Nobel Prize for Literature in 1967, is one of the first academic racists, openly publi-
cizing his rejection of the indigenous people in his thesis about
the social problem of the indigenous people.

Discrimination exists in all fields of the government system. We can see it in Congress, in the school system, in the bank
system, and so on. More than 50% of the positions are held by
Ladinos. However, it has changed after the signing of the peace
accords in 1996 as compared to previous years. When I was in
elementary school and then in high school, 90% of my teachers were non-indigenous; in university they all were Ladinos.

What they called 'Model Villages' were used to massacre
poor peasants. This system was also used in Vietnam by the U.S.
In these villages the people spoke different languages and...it
was difficult for them to understand each other in order to get
organized.

. . . .

Researchers have described the effects of violence and civil war
on Maya children's ethnic identity. In the *Handbook of Action Research,* Margarita Melville and M. Brinton Lykes distinguish be-

tween trauma experienced by populations affected by war waged
by a foreign force and those affected by civil war:

> When war is waged by a hostile, foreign force, the
> members of a community can utilize their national
> and/or ethnic identity to rally their members in
> self-defense. When civil war is waged...the clear
> identification of the enemy...is more problematic.
> And when a population faces government-spon-
> sored terrorism, human rights and due process of
> law are suspended by the very institutions claiming
> to be their guardians.

The struggle to maintain Maya identity within the dominant
culture is a recurring theme. In the following testimonio, Robin describes having to negotiate between two identities, his Maya identity and that as a member of the larger society. This can emerge in
the most seemingly insignificant moments: one morning he took
me on a tour of the market in Guatemala City. I saw a tee shirt with
100% CHAPIN emblazoned across the front and asked "What does
that mean, Chapin?"

"It's a nickname for Guatemalans," he said. "It means, we're all
Guatemalans. But, for me, I don't know. Some Maya want to wear
it, but others not."

. . . .

> "To explain my feelings in detail is painful. Because
> this country is very hard on indigenous people.
> This war...was always against indigenous people."
> —Robin

ROBIN'S WAR

Robin is a 25-year-old Achi' Maya man studying engineering
at the University of San Carlos. Like Hélida and Mateo, he talks

about the sometimes blurry line between who is Maya and who Ladino. He described the breakdown of community ties that was a result of chaos and violence. And it was important to Robin that I understand that, in reality, there wasn't ever a *war*, because the indigenous people did not have weapons. Just as Víctor had explained, the Maya were caught between the guerrillas and the army, innocent citizens persecuted by their own government.

I think that in Guatemala a war didn't really exist. Because my people, the *indígenas* (indigenous people), didn't have weapons. The government had weapons, vehicles, helicopters. The guerrillas lived in the mountains near my town, and they came into town to buy food. And the government saw the guerrillas and tried to capture them. It was very hard to catch them, and the government killed many people (who were not guerrillas).

And anywhere the government attacked, there was a great deal of confusion, and during the confusion the townspeople stole from each other, they stole cows and other things. They were envious of each other. The men were jealous. If they saw a woman they liked, they took advantage of the confusion.

My mother and father escaped and went to Cobán for five years and then moved to the City, because they were afraid to go back to our town. But it was very difficult to live in the City, because we don't have a house, don't have objects you need to live, a bed, a table. It was difficult to pay rent. My mother worked in the market selling vegetables and fruits. I always helped my mother when I was little. I went with her house-to-house, carrying two baskets. I sold toys.

I always was curious about the electronic toys. I thought that I would make toys when I was grown up. I was curious about what was inside the toys, so I would take them apart. My mother always says, 'No, no, no!' This is the reason that I study electronics at the University.

56

This country is very hard on the indigenous people. The war delayed our development. They only want Ladinos to become prosperous. So, for example, in the government, they are always Ladinos. The owners of companies are foreigners or Ladinos. The indigenous people work the land, and their vegetables and fruits are sent to foreign countries. But the Ladinos do the exporting. Indigenous people always work, work, work. The only thing we can do is fight our way forward. But I think now we are changing a little bit, because now there are professional indigenous people.

For me there exist two groups of people: first, the people in this scholarship program. They are very, very good friends, because we're equal. We have many experiences in common and there's a lot of understanding. But in the university it's different. There are just two indígenas in my class. But you can't always tell if they are indígenas or Ladinos. I have one friend, he's a very good friend, and we understand each other, but we don't talk about the problems. Once I asked him if he was Maya and he was, and it was excellent to have this opportunity to get to know him. But with the Ladinos, even though I feel equal, it's hard, because they don't always treat you as an equal.

For example, I had an experience a year ago. I was at the university with my girlfriend, Griselda, who is Maya. She wears the traje. And I met a friend, a classmate, and when he saw me, he made a noise: 'pswwsshh', (like he was disgusted). Afterwards, when he saw me he didn't ever really talk to me.

· · · · · · ·

Hurt and anger at pervasive racism and the denigrating attitudes of the dominant culture infuse the testimonios given by Hélida, Mateo, and Robin. They actively resist discrimination by continuing to speak their Maya language and by wearing the traditional traje, expressing pride in their Maya identity.

Robin's story about his classmate's reaction to Griselda's traje is one example of a response to the seemingly insignificant matter of dress. The matter of identity being expressed by clothing has few direct corallaries in US culture, but in Guatemala clothing is of crucial importance as explained by authors Margarita Melville and M. Brinton Lykes in the *Handbook of Action Research*.

> Traditionally, women have been more resistant to put aside traditional community-specific clothing, while men more easily adopted simple peasant trousers and shirts for everyday wear, leaving it to their wives and daughters to maintain the family's community identity in regards to dress. Where deprivation of both dress and language occurs, it represents the loss of an important ethnic identity and symbol, the mechanism for maintaining community solidarity.

. . . .

> "I want you to call me Balam, which means jaguar in my Maya language. Someday I hope to get a job in the government and I don't want anything I say to you to be used against me. I want to tell my story, the story of Maya young people, but I'm not sure how safe it is here even now."
> —Balam

BALAM'S WAR

Balam is a 25-year-old Poqomchi' Maya man studying international relations at the University of San Carlos. He was the first person who talked to me about childhood experiences during the violence. When I heard Balam's story I wondered if it were somehow exaggerated and dramatized to engender sympathy. After listening to many similiar stories of deprivation, disruption and devastating loss I came to understand that this first story I heard had all the elements of every other I would hear. It was, in fact, *the* story. Balam requested that I use a pseudonym for him, because, ten years after the peace, he still does not feel safe using his real name. Like Robin, Balam describes the often fluid line between identifying oneself as Maya or Ladino. He stresses the importance of the traje to Maya women, and his commitment to continuing to speak his Maya language. He describes how fear can erode identity, how sometimes Maya "act like Ladinos" to protect themselves and their children.

I can tell if someone is Maya or Ladino, because I can just sense it. Sometimes Maya people try to act more like Ladinos. Some professional Maya women do not dress the traditional way. It's cheaper to wear 'normal' clothes than to wear Mayan, because we have to make them, and if we cannot, we have to buy, but it costs thousands of *quetzales.* It's very expensive, and we don't have enough money to buy even food. That's why some people try to use cheap clothes for their children. But the children grow up with these clothes, and then their mentality is not Maya anymore. Because if they wear pants or jeans, then they see in the shops and they want to buy that, they are more automatically, they are...being like Ladinos. They are Ladinos. But sometimes they don't think about it, they just do it. They don't think it's good, or not good, they just do it.

At the university 99% of the students are Ladino. I can tell who the Maya students are, but not everyone can tell. But the thing is, we don't talk about our culture. We know, we feel Maya, but we are, in Spanish we say, *bloqueado* (shut down).

But we act like Ladinos, because we are afraid, and we grow up with this mentality from our parents. They are thinking to teach us Spanish when we are small, because they don't want us to suffer. They want us to survive, to be happy.

But if I have children I will teach them my language. But I am one in a thousand Maya, because I think like this, because I recognize the value of culture and I have investigated our origins, what we did in the past. We are totally different than what we would have been, without the Spanish, the army and being forced to become slaves. We didn't have time in 500 years, to grow our science, our knowledge, our spirituality, because it was cut, cut, cut!

We invented the zero, and the Europeans didn't have the zero at that time. So we have an exact calendar. We have mathematics and science. Even now I don't know a lot about my culture. I live here, and I still don't understand many things.

Ever since I was a little kid I didn't play games or anything. I started working when I was five years old. I was a little farmer. And after that I was with my grandmother in the little shop she had in the market. We were traveling, buying things from one place to another one, and we were surviving like this. Later I had a stepfather, and he didn't like us, and he put me and my sister on the farm. She was a farmer, working like a man when she was little. He would separate us, I was about a kilometer from my sister at another place in the mountain. And I have trauma because I saw snakes or something, and I was scared, because I was only five years old.

We could plant our food, but we had to work for these Ladinos who give us a piece of land to live, but we had to work from 6:00 in the morning to 6:00 in the evening, without lunch. I only have my breakfast and my dinner. That is why I am so small! This is still happening in Guatemala, with millions of Maya people.

I first went to school when I was nine. I didn't speak Spanish. The teachers were Ladino, they prohibited us from speaking our language in school. We started laughing with each other, but we were not permitted to speak Poqomchi'. We had to speak Spanish without knowing any words. We have classes in Spanish, and we didn't understand, and if we don't understand they hit you on the head with a ruler.

I went to school only because my grandmother did everything she possibly could to send me to school. But my sister and brother didn't go because they didn't have any money to send them. When I was little my grandmother said that she could not pay any more for my studies. She asked me to find a job. So I went to ask in different private schools and public schools if I can continue going to school and how much money it cost every month. But at the end of the last year of grammar school, the principal of my school, he asked me—it was like an accident or a miracle—and he asked me, 'Where do you live? What is your name?' Because he didn't know me because we were 1,500 students in that school. So in that moment he asked me where I live, who were my parents. And I say, 'I don't have parents' and then he offered me a job working with a dentist.

I needed to eat, I needed to study, I needed to pay for school. The principal was also looking for a scholarship for me, because my grades were high. I got a half-scholarship, but they only gave me the school fees, I had to pay my uniform, my books, everything else.

Later I got a job in a laboratory, and also in a photography studio, and I ask them not to pay me, just to give me food, and I will see where I can find some money, just 'give me food and I will work for free'. And they accepted. But they did not want me to become a professional. So they fire me. After one month, they say, 'Now we cannot give you food, so you have to leave. You don't have a job anymore.' So then I cannot pay for my studies, I did not have any food, and then I had to live on the streets again.

I have lived by myself since I was eleven years old. I had a teacher who asked me to go to live with his family, that they could help me and give me food, 'Because you are a good student, you should finish your career.' But I felt so—how do you say?—without dignity, like they were insulting me too much. They weren't! But I took it like that. I didn't accept, I said, 'Thank you, thank you very much, but I have hands, I am smart, and I can work to find a job. I love to learn and to be a student, and thank you for offering to help me. But I think I'm going to change my life, right now.'

So I took my stuff and I left school. I left Cobán and came to Antigua. I cried for four hours from Cobán to Antigua. Then I got work here. I thought maybe I could find a job with some organization because I speak two Mayan languages, and Spanish and also at that time I learned a little bit of French and English. I finished high school by correspondence. I started at the university in 2002; I'm studying International Relations. I like it because it's very complete, because you know a little bit of everything of the world, economics, countries, everything.

I have had a lot of friends from Europe, but I didn't have Maya friends. I used to when I was small in Cobán, but when I came here everything changed. I wanted to know Europeans, the white people, how they think, how they see the world, what they think about the Maya, and you discover that they see things totally different than we do. Maybe it's normal. I cannot tell the white person about their own culture, and it's the same thing with me. They just can think something about us, but they don't know us. Tourists come here for vacation, not to learn. They take pictures and that's all, like it's an exotic thing. How do the tourists think they can understand it in a few months?

Some white people grew up with this anger, this racism. They hate the Maya. They think we are ugly, they think we are nothing and they want to live in a country without us. They were taught to be angry, taught to hate. And then they were shown, 'You can do this. They are nothing, they are Indians, they are the enemy to hate.' This is how they were brainwashed. Then they get crazy. This to me is not normal.

These attitudes still exist. When we go to the modern part of the City, they say, 'Ewww, this city, this part is not good anymore. Because there are Indians here.' And that tells you they hate us. One time I went to a modern discotheque with one of my friends, and they didn't let us in. They say, 'No, you cannot come in, you have to come with formal dresses.' But my friend, she had on formal and expensive Mayan clothes. Because we have different clothes from what you use every day and from what you wear to a party, they are higher quality and expensive. She was dressed very elegant, and they didn't let her in, just because she was Maya. A woman can be a doctor, lawyer, anything, and she can be treated like that, just because she is Maya.

During the violence the army tortured the women, they cut their breasts, and if a woman was pregnant they just took the baby, and then they killed them. They did things you don't imagine that anyone could do. The Maya soldiers who were in the army were forced to do these things. You know, some young people, they committed suicide after they did this. Afterwards they just couldn't keep living.

Finally we are starting to write the history now. The people who did these things are still there, the army is still there, the government is still there, and the victims are here, but they are afraid to talk. The real truth is here, but there are only a few books where they talk about what really happened.

· · · · · · ·

In the *Handbook of Action Research*, Melville and Lykes emphasize the vital importance of ethnic identity in maintaining a sense of self. "Ethnic identity and knowing one's roots can be viewed as an anchor for mental health in a world disintegrating around them [children]." This is precisely what is threatened when Balam tells about being hit in school for speaking his Maya language; precisely what Robin describes when his friend at the university rejects him after seeing Griselda wearing traje.

Racism is not solely a set of discrete acts or behaviors, but rather an all-enveloping reality, an accepted part of everyday life which permeates a culture. It is profoundly felt and understood by those it targets. It often remains ignored and invisible to those who perpetuate it, who live believing that it is "the natural order of things."

Racism, discrimination, the learned hate that Balam calls "brainwashing:" these are all part of the daily existence of these young Maya. Hélida, Mateo, Robin, and Balam describe different aspects of the same reality, and although their experiences differ, they are all resisting the subtle, as well as the overt, efforts to force them to assimilate. They are aware that this effort to eradicate their indigenous culture has its roots in the Spanish conquest. By resisting they participate in the long thread of Maya history, so aptly called "our culture is our resistance" by Jonathan Moeller. (See his book of photographs, *Our Culture is Our Resistance, Repression, Refuge, and Healing in Guatemala*, NY: Powerhouse Books, (2004.)

6
Severed Roots

> "To be rooted is perhaps the most important and least recognized need of the human soul."
>
> —Simone Weil

IN *THE NEED FOR ROOTS*, philospher Simone Weil discusses the human need for multiple connections. Although she was writing about France in the 1940s, she could just as easily have been describing Guatemala.

> A human being has roots by virtue of his real, active, and natural participation in the life of a community, which preserves in living shape certain particular treasures of the past and certain particular expectations for the future."

In the following testimonios, Pancho, Bartolo, and Ical grieve not only for the homes left behind, but also for the sense of home. Houses, cooking utensils, a way of life, and family pets had to be abandoned. Ical, a young husband, offers this vignette: "My wife's family still remember their dog who was very good, but they had to leave him. According to the *Popol Vuh* and Maya history, relationships with animals are very important. I see my wife and mother-in-law crying when they mention the dog and they say that because of the armed conflict they had to leave him and they don't know what happened to him. Whatever happened to those poor animals! There is much sadness for the father (who was killed), but also for the house, the family, the animals."

Although this disruption of the "natural participation in the life of a community" happened to one degree or another to all Maya survivors, these testimonios about severed roots differ from those in the previous chapter because Pancho and Bartolo's families were forced to flee Guatemala. They grew up in refugee camps in Mexico and in their testimonios we come to understand the ways that this displacement altered their lives irrevocably.

> "I still have the desire for revenge, not with violence, but to demonstrate that even when we were forced to leave, we could not be destroyed."
> —Pancho

PANCHO'S WAR

Pancho is a 31-year-old K'iche' Maya man finishing his degree in communications at the University of San Carlos. His family fled to Mexico during the violence. Although they returned to Guatemala, he says that they have not been able to return to their community. He considers himself the only person in his family who retains a Maya identity.

My name is Francisco, but I'm called Pancho. I was five during the worst part of the war. I don't remember a lot, I didn't live the war directly, but through recollections from my parents and grandparents I have recovered a little of that story. When I was a child, I didn't know what was happening. However, at age five, something happened which

Pancho

affected me a lot. Now, I feel vulnerable and have many ups and downs, which makes it difficult for people to understand me. My uncles told me the story of what happened the day they came to get my grandfather and took him away. I lost my grandfather to the war. It was very hard for our family, and it left a mark on the whole town, because my grandfather was a *catequista* (lay religious teacher), a leader. Maybe that was the motive to kidnap him.

I didn't grow up in the same place where I was born, and it is very difficult when you go back and realize that this doesn't really feel like home anymore. I was a refugee in Mexico for 20 years. My cultural identity is not Guatemalan, and it's been very difficult to reclaim my identity and my customs. And this has also fragmented my family.

Most of my brothers don't consider themselves Guatemalan, they consider themselves Mexican citizens. Even though they are my brothers, there are still those differences between them and me. I am involved in working with the indigenous people, with our ideology, culture, and the Maya way of thinking. However, my brothers are not. I wouldn't say that they think like Ladinos, but still, they aren't knowledgeable about Maya culture. They were born and raised in a different environment (in Mexico). They probably never understood what happened to our people, and that's sad.

I recognize that in my family all my uncles, my parents, understood the conflict from a different perspective. They were guerrillas up to the moment of the peace signing. They always were, but now they don't even know what they are. They have so much inner turmoil that they can't sort things out. For instance, we, the whole family, cannot return to our community, because in that town they see us as guilty for the violence, which has been very difficult.

I'm the only one who has returned to Santa Cruz del Quiché, that lives here permanently. The rest of my family lives in Escuintla. That's why I don't even really know where I'm from. My grandma asked me if I had ever gone back to the town, to our house, because she heard that there was some furniture still there. When she came back to Guatemala in 1998 after being a refugee, the first thing she looked for was her grinding stone. She found it and her burned armoire. Her house was burned, the only thing left were the walls. I think my relatives live in the past, even now, remembering many things: the stones, the pots, the sewing machines, many things that were needed at home, they remember them and they miss them.

I have a son, Fernando, and I don't talk to him about the war yet (because he's too young). However, I think the reality is going to catch up with him the first time he goes to the old house where I was born and raised. I think he will sense it there because that house is not like the ones we have here, which are better ones. (I think it's important that) he learn about our culture. We must keep it alive.

It's very difficult to try to understand someone else. I do therapy to myself. I told you about when I'm riding the bus and I think of my grandfather; suddenly I'm just crying. I have gotten used to not being embarrassed of people seeing my tears because it happens a lot to me. And I may be wrong, but with everything that I do, I'm always thinking 'Grandpa, help me.' It's something that is there despite the fact that I only knew him for five years. Many things remind me of him. Sometimes it hurts a lot.

In the case of my grandpa who disappeared, for many years his family—my father and my uncles—they never did anything, like excavating, exhumation, or research about what had happened to him. They haven't dared to do it until now. Recently however, they got together to ask (the authorities) if he could be found.

At the university I'm studying communication sciences, and that's what I like, but I also think it's important because the media has a great capacity to transform realities and many young people need to express ourselves. We need to be understood. For example, there isn't much information about our Maya culture. We need to let other people know about us.

I have written about these things, and I still have the desire for revenge, not with violence, but to demonstrate that even when we were forced to leave, we could not be destroyed. It's not that I want ugly revenge, but I feel the pain, and that's what the conflict has left us.

That's mostly what I have to tell. Thank you for the opportunity.

. . . .

Many people who gave testimonios said that in the past they had not felt safe talking about their experiences, and so, had remained silent. Melville and Lykes speak to this point. "Inside Guatemala children were more frequently urged to keep silence, lest the telling of their stories be overheard by *orejas* (spies) and further endanger themselves or their families."

However, children who were displaced and grew up in refugee camps in Mexico often had a different experience: "In the refugee camps these incidents are often retold in the evenings as the group sits together in the candlelight before retiring. It is impossible to tell how much these children remember on their own and how much the story, elaborated by the group as a whole, has become part of their general recollection."

. . . .

"When we were in Mexico, I remember the first days, it was a difficult situation...what I remember most is when they made the women change their clothes, because no one wanted them to wear their typical dress because the Guatemalan military came (looking for us) there."

—Bartolo

BARTOLO'S WAR

Bartolo is another young man who talks about being uprooted. He was also a refugee in Mexico for many years. When his father decided to return to Guatemala, Bartolo did not want to go. He describes the experience of returning to a home that did not feel like home, a place where he felt like a stranger. Bartolo is a 25 year old Chuj Maya man finishing his law degree at the University of San Carlos.

In Yalambojoch, the village where I was born, many people were killed. The army killed my mother. My father, my brothers and I fled into the mountains; we walked for three days to get to Mexico. We walked all day and all night, and we hid from the army. In Mexico we lived in one house with lots of other peo-

ple. The houses were very close together. I finished the third grade, and then I learned to make shoes and jewelry and I was studying printing.

We returned in 1993. My father came back to Guatemala because he is a leader, an important person who organized people. We gathered in the city of Comitán in Mexico, and on the 20th of January we left there and crossed the border and came into

Bartolo

Guatemala. We slept that night in Huehuetenango. I was thirteen years old, and I was very sad, because I did not want to come. I was very happy in Mexico, and I wasn't accustomed to Guatemala. Our old village did not exist, it had been burned, so there was a new village called *Víctoria 20 de enero* (Víctoria the 20th of January), because that was the date that the first group of refugees returned. But my uncles never came back to Guatemala because they were scared.

In Mexico, yes, I talked a lot about this, but we talked only with other refugees. But it's sad, it's painful. So I don't talk about it regularly. Because sometimes, the people who talk a lot, the ones who tell their stories, they might be killed. So, it's better not to talk to people you're not sure about.

But now I am happy to live in Guatemala. I am a Guatemalan citizen. I'm expecting to receive my diploma in law. What is most important is for us to rise above what happened, to be professionals now. I think that we, the professionals, we are going to be the ones who make the difference in the future.

As we said goodbye, Bartolo gave me a poem that he had written on January 20th, 2003, the 10th anniversary of the founding of his village.

El Refugio	*The Refuge*
Por la guerra huí	Because of the war I fled
atemorizado llegué.	In fear I arrived
por tu ayuda crecí.	Because of your help I grew,
Salvaste mi vida,	You saved my life,
Curaste mi herida,	You healed my wound,
Por ti, existo	Because of you, I exist
Gracias México	Thank you Mexico

Simone Weil describes the interplay between place and particiation in the life of the community that is:

> ...natural in the sense that it is automatically brought about by place, conditions of birth, profession, and social surroundings. Every human being needs to have multiple roots. It is necessary for him to draw well-nigh the whole of his moral, intellectual, and spiritual life by way of the environment of which he forms a natural part.

In a private conversation, theologian Susan J. White, observed:

> These narratives describe the interruption of the child's moral, intellectual, and spiritual way of life. Loss is the overarching theme: the loss of the 'real, active, and natural participation in the life of a community'; the loss of a sense that the past, present, and future are connected and have a discernible trajectory; loss of the sense that one occupies the same universe as those who went before and those yet to come. So when Pancho says that he doesn't 'really know where (he's) from' he is speaking about more than just being wrenched from a particular place, but, rather from a whole web of social and historical associations."

Pancho, Bartolo, and Ical tell us about their loss of home, their loss of a sense of being home, or even being able to return home. Home is gone.

7
One Family

THE EXPERIENCE OF WAR IS NEVER GENERIC; every survivor tells a different story. Even within one family each person experiences the trauma of violence in his or her own unique way, determined by age, gender, role in the family, and political affiliations. Three months after my meeting with the students, I returned to Guatemala to travel in the Altiplano and to collect more testimonies. I stayed at the home of one of the students where I spoke with his mother, uncle and grandfather.

The family members requested that they be identified not by name but by their relationship to Carlos, their 30-year-old relative, who had disappeared in 1985. When Carlos disappeared his oldest son was six years old. His wife was terrified, grief-stricken, and alone with four young children. His brother joined the guerrillas, remaining in Mexico even after peace was declared. His father lost two sons and his son-in-law and any shred of trust in the government. In spite of the danger, his anger and despair compelled him to go to the capital to confront government officials, demanding in-

73

formation about his murdered family. The *REHMI Report* describes this crisis in this way:

> Countless families were wrenched from the reality they had known their entire lives; this crisis demanded new survival strategies. Families faced the dilemma of fleeing to save their lives, fully aware that if they did so, the army would accuse them of being members of the guerrillas. (They) were faced with the paradox in which any decision they made could imperil their lives.

The testimonios that follow are from these four family members who describe events that occurred more than twenty years before, affecting each of them in profoundly different ways.

. . . .

"Many feel like crying, and cannot speak. But now, I need to know more about this."

—Carlos's son

CARLOS'S SON'S WAR

Carlos's son is a 25 year old Kaqchikel Maya man studying architecture at the University of San Carlos. As he listened to his uncle and grandfather give their testimonios, he heard parts of his father's story that he had never been told.

I want to talk with you about the history of the conflict in my town. Many people were murdered, in my family, but not only my family. Many people have problems; they still have problems, even though this conflict happened many years ago. I don't understand why it happened. I don't understand what it had to do with the people. The people were very poor, they didn't understand politics. Many people died and never knew why.

One problem is that many people think the Maya people are inferior, and the political problems were one justification to kill them. Another justification (they used was) to end Communism which was attributed to the indigenous people. But, this was only a pretext to kill them.

The people in the villages had a lot of fear, they were scared of the army and the guerrillas. Many people became guerrillas because they saw that the army was killing people. And, of course, the guerrillas don't do anything to you, they are like friends, you are looking for someone to help you. So, what do you do? But I would say that many, many of the people didn't know the difference between who were the guerrillas and who were the army. Really, I don't sympathize with any of them.

I remember conversations, one time between my grandpa and my mother and father and uncles. My grandfather said he had two people who worked for him and one time these two men turned up dead. He said it was the army (that killed them). The men had machetes that were for planting and whoever killed them made a cross with the machetes on their chests. I don't know, to me, it's like making fun of the people that died.

People said that my father was a guerrilla, the same as my uncles were, but my father wasn't. He was a nurse, he worked in the health center, and traveled around to visit sick people in the countryside. Maybe this was interpreted as though he was going around talking—I don't know—about political things.

My father was working in the city when he disappeared. That day four people disappeared: my father, his brother-in-law and two others. One month later my uncle also disappeared. The army searched for him in his house and they grabbed him. Altogether, in my family, my father and my two uncles disappeared. My other uncle was afraid the same thing would happen to him, and he went to seek refuge in Mexico. My mother and us kids were persecuted and went into hiding, first in our town. We hid in different houses, and then we went to Guatemala City, to run away for a time.

I knew my father had disappeared because I heard all the people talking, and I understood. But my mother never spoke about all this. Even today she never cried in front of us. I don't know, maybe it was to protect us, but she didn't ever tell us about all that had happened. Never. My mother never told us, 'You poor children.' She just worked. She's an elementary school teacher. She was go, go, go! She is very strong in her mind. Now she says that it was so we wouldn't feel hate. My mother would never say, 'Your father was killed by the army.' She believed that if she told us, my siblings and I, we would grow up with hate. Since we were so young, she wanted to keep us from becoming bitter. If my mother had told me all that had happened, it might have affected my mind, I might have believed that my father would come back. My grandparents believe that my father and uncle will come back. They look for him still.

I don't talk about this because there's too many people who don't understand how I...maybe I'm wrong, but we have very different points of view. Many people even today they feel a lot of hate. They say 'I am poor because I suffered a lot.' I understand that this has happened, that it wasn't right, that it wasn't just, but it doesn't do any good to feel that kind of hate. I think it's better to work hard, to study hard.

I haven't talked to many people about all of this. There are many stories that are much sadder, and much more complicated than mine. Many people cry when they talk about this. But I don't remember crying for my father. But it's good when I talk about this, sometimes I remember other parts, and it makes me feel better. With my uncles, my grandma, my grandpa, my mother, I've never asked questions. But now I feel...I know the history, what the books say, but now I feel like I am ready to ask questions. Before I didn't feel ready to hear all this. I haven't been able to talk to them until now, because each time we talk about this, they cry. Many feel like crying and cannot speak, but now I need to know more. I need to know, I need to ask what my mother feels, what my uncle feels now. Many years after, maybe now they've come to terms with it. And my feelings are more mature. My younger brothers and sister aren't interested and the interest has to come from them. Maybe they won't want to talk about it, maybe they feel like they still can't. Maybe they feel the same way I did, that they aren't ready for this.

I have more memories of my father than my younger siblings do, but the memories I have are not clear. I only have two photos of him. There were many photographs, but during the time of the violence, my mother burned or buried them because she was afraid that someone would see them, and they would probably go and look for us.

There is one other way I remember my father. When I was eight or ten I found a sheet of paper, and I didn't know what it was. I read, 'kitchen, bathroom, living room'…this is a plan, one small page where there is a design of a house. I asked my mother, 'What is this?' and she told me that my father wanted to build this house for the family. I don't know, but in this moment maybe I felt that I wanted to study this. I asked myself how they had done each of the little drawings, the trees, the chairs, the tables. I could already imagine the house. And I still have this design.

So I finished elementary school, and I wanted to study architecture. I never veered, I knew this was what I wanted. I don't know, to me this house excited me very much. Now I look at the design and feel, perhaps the same as I did as a child. And just the same, the drawing is bad!

Now I know this was a dream of my father's. My father had many dreams. He wanted this house. Maybe I can make one dream of my father's. I want to build this house in two or three years. His house. Sometimes when I remember my father I don't feel like crying, I feel happy.

The son, my former student, had invited me to stay with his family. He had explained that his mother had never discussed her experiences with him. I was reluctant to intrude and had not yet decided whether to ask Carlos's widow if she wanted to be interviewed. Still uncertain, and exhausted after my flight, I was half-asleep when she appeared at the doorway of the room, and then sat down on the bed beside me. She didn't say anything, so I waited. Finally, I asked, "Señora, do you want to tell your story?"

The *REHMI Report* describes the effect on women after their husbands were murdered or disappeared. "Women had to cope alone and see to the material and emotional survival of their families....difficult circumstances have led to increased recognition of women's worth and authority as heads of family."

. . . .

"I dreamed every day about my husband. And one
day, since I was going crazy, I said I would go and
look for him because he's not dead."
—Carlos's widow

CARLOS'S WIDOW'S WAR

Carlos's widow is a 49-year-old Kaqchikel Maya woman, whose life was wrenched apart when her husband disappeared. While he was alive, she stayed home with their four children, fulfilling the traditional roles of a Maya woman. After his disappearance she struggled with profound grief and despair. She had been a homemaker, now she had to go back to school, earn a degree, find a job, provide for her children. Initially, she taught elementary school. Now she translates children's books from Spanish into Kaqchikel. She starts by saying that she felt she was "going crazy" when her husband disappeared. Not knowing what happened to him, and not being able to give him a proper burial, intensified her profound loss.

Carlos was thirty when he disappeared, I was twenty-eight. I had the four kids, one son was six years old, my daughter was four, the other one was two, and I had just had the baby. When the kids asked me questions I told them we couldn't go with Dad. When they were very young I told them that. But, when they were a little older, I told them their dad wasn't here, that we didn't know what happened to him, that maybe he died. And if he died, we have to behave very well to go with him someday. The one who suffered and knew his dad well was our oldest son.

Carlos would take the oldest boy to his job with him. He said, 'I'll buy him toys and he'll be with me.' And it happened like that many times. And so he felt his dad's absence and now he says he remembers him, but his memories are vague. The others don't remember him at all.

And one day, since I was going crazy, I said I would go and look for him because he's not dead. Maybe I was weak or sick, and I started walking with the idea that I'd find him. My mother-in-law followed me and asked me where I was going. I told her to the store, but it was 5:00 in the morning. So she told me that nothing was open. Then I went to the doctor and he said that if I couldn't accept what had happened, I would go crazy and there were already many at the asylum.

I got frightened because I had my kids, I had to fight, and I'd cry then at night, so that they wouldn't see me, and I'd ask God to help me fill that emptiness I had in my heart. And then, I went to my mother and she made a *ruda* cup of tea (a natural antidepressant) for me. That helped me. The doctor had said that he'd give sedatives, but that I would get used to them at some point, and they wouldn't help anymore. I decided I'd rather pray to God to help me, because it was terrible, four kids, what was I to do?

When my husband was alive there was always that help, we both worked. Carlos was a very good father. He was responsible. For instance, when the children were sick, he would make the decisions, we were two people working together. But when I was left alone, I had to figure things out on my own, and if I didn't have the money, I had to find it. When he was here, he'd do that, so that short time was good for me. Then, it was hard because one way or the other I had to solve any health or school problems. But, after he was gone, it was terrible for me. But I really thank God because He helped me forget him since it has been already twenty years. It's not the same as it was when it had just happened.

Later, I was working as a teacher in San José, and it was terrible there, too. There were people with covered faces arriving, taking people from their homes, killing them at the market and when I went on the bus they would look at you and at pictures they were carrying...It was terrible and many people died, even entire families, kids, parents, and I thought that we were lucky not to have been with my husband, or we would have all been caught. God knows.

Thank God that I decided that I didn't want another man, I didn't want to marry again, I would be with my children and I'd work for them. Because another man might love me, but not my children. So, I said no, no, no. I worked, then I went to the university, I got a scholarship, and studied for three more years to be a teacher, then two more, which means I was very busy. That helped me because before that I was like a broken record, dreaming every night about my husband.

We lived together only eight years. Carlos was very friendly, everybody said that. He always said, 'Good morning, good-bye.' And he also had that desire to help. He said that he'd help whenever he could. And for instance, my daughter's husband, he sometimes says: 'Let's go have fun' and he invites us to join him. But I tell him, 'No, keep your money because you may need it.' But my daughter says that he's like that, giving, and that is good, too. And Carlos was like that; he had a big heart, he talked and laughed. That's how he was, friendly, smiling.

And I know it's hard alone with the kids, but they have turned out good, they don't have bad habits, and I keep telling them that we have to believe in God because that is very important. Because there are families with the mom and dad and the children are into bad habits, so I'm thankful to my mother and everybody because they have supported us, and I'm with my children now. Many people ask me why I didn't get married again, they said my children would get married and leave, and I'd be alone again. But I think, I don't want another man because he's not going to love my children. And I thank God because I was able to survive that difficult time.

When my oldest son and my daughter finished third grade, they had to go to the capital to study, and I didn't make enough money. So, I decided to change jobs to get another one that paid a little more. At that time, teachers didn't earn much. Well, they graduated from high school, but I told them they have to go on to the university. Then, when my son was in his third year studying architecture, I told him that I couldn't help him anymore because I had to help his brothers, too. So, he looked for a scholarship. I talked to the people at Fundación para los Estudios y Profesionalización Maya (FEPMaya) who suggested he send his application. That's when he started being helped, thanks to all of you. Now, my other two children are just starting at the university and I tell them to follow their brother's example because he would stay in on Saturdays and Sundays studying, he wouldn't sleep all night. He is very committed, and, thank God, he is almost finished.

So, I have these two other sons that I'm trying to get through the university because it's not enough just to have a high school diploma. And I tell my children that, thank God, they graduated because there are many mothers that couldn't afford to send their kids to school. Even though my salary was not much, I had enough to pay for education and I thank God for everything He has given us because we have gotten ahead, even though we don't have everything. I have spent most of my money for education, even though we don't have many clothes, because there are families with a lot of money and clothes and cars, but they don't have an education. My daughter got married, and I'm happy with the other three.

And I tell the children that life is short, we should love each other, we are here today, but we may not be tomorrow. That's how life is, with so many dangers, and I always tell them that we go to church and that respect for God helps us not to do bad things, mainly because we may die tomorrow, and it's not good to die in sin.

Well, that all happened, but it was twenty years ago. Yes, it's sad. But my children are already grown, I have grandchildren, time goes by fast. I can't forget, but time helps to not feel the same pain.

Thank you so much, also for knowing you. And now, rest, because it's late.

Carlos's widow and many bereaved family members attempted to find their loved one's body to provide a proper burial. Melville and Lykes refer to "the cultural importance that the Maya place on burying the dead near their ancestral villages:"

The disappearance of an individual is particularly disruptive to the web of family and social life because of the uncertainty, fear, and near paralysis it creates. For the Mayans, who harbor a deep religious respect for the deceased and a belief in the need for the souls of their dead to rest in or near their ancestral villages, the unknown whereabouts of relatives, alive or dead, causes immense distress and disrupts the ability to perform normal routines.

Carlos's widow never remarried. In *The Quiet Revolutionaries,* authors Frank Afflitto and Paul Jesilow explain that "to remarry would have been to deny one's culture, to deny one's own identity and existence but most importantly to deny the existence of the disappeared. The value of family is forever. Just as one does not replace his or her children if they are missing, one does not replace a husband who is missing but still 'with' the family." This has been Carlos's widow's lived experience.

Carlos's brother is the only surviving son in his family. He joined the guerrillas during the early 1980s; he described four different guerrilla groups. When I asked about the number of guerrilla fighters he estimated that there were 15,000. In *Of Centaurs and Doves, Guatemala's Peace Process,* Suzanne Jonas states that during 1980–1981 when the guerrilla forces were at their largest, there were between 6,000–8,000 armed fighters, and 250,000–500,000 active collaborators and supporters. In all likelihood, it was difficult to determine exactly who was a guerrilla and who a supporter. Carlos's son listened to his uncle's testimonio, and heard part of his uncle's history and his father's story he had never been told before.

. . . .

"If I had physical strength, I would join the fight again."
—Carlos's brother

CARLOS'S BROTHER'S WAR

When I joined the guerrillas, I did it totally, I could not leave, because I had come to understand the effects of poverty and injustice in our lives. I also realized some other things about the United States intervention in the war and the (history of the) overthrow of Arbenz, back in 1954 when the United Fruit Company intervened (in our internal affairs). I started to realize all of this—so our objective was not just to overthrow the army, but to get rid of foreign intervention from gringos. We also recognized that during the time of John F. Kennedy's presidency that people were sent from the Peace Corps with the purpose of finding out who the insurgents were. The U.S. wanted a totalitarian, military government, while we wanted a civil government, a democratic government.

The guerrillas fought the Guatemalan army with whatever weapons we had. We were trying to save the civilian population because the army would come to kill, to massacre, mostly in El Quiché, Quetzaltenango, San Marcos, Huehuetenango and the Central Altiplano. Those are the places that were taken by the army. I was there for three or four years around the Quiché area.

The soldiers would arrive, and just because someone was a cathequista, or the president of a co-op, they were accused of being with the guerrillas. The townspeople suffered. Most of all, they suffered. While we, those of us in the mountains were not as affected, because the army knew we were going to fight back.

Of course, when we reached a town, not everybody wanted to become involved in the fighting. Others, often young people of fourteen, fifteen, up to twenty-five, whose father, mother, or children had been killed, they were very angry. So they joined us. We attacked the army, and we tried to leave some resistance in the towns.

Unfortunately, the army came with more sophisticated

weapons, like airplanes and tanks. They would kill everyone. So even when the guerrillas tried to take over the Central Altiplano, we couldn't do it because the U.S. intervened militarily and financially by sending military advisors to the Guatemalan army to help them fight against the guerrillas. So General Rios Montt started to kill anybody.

We felt the consequences in the mountains, we were in the open, without houses, and sometimes we ran out of weapons, so we had to quit fighting.

There were about 15,000 Guatemalan guerrillas. About 99.5% were indigenous and only .5% Ladinos. One major problem was that the leaders were Ladinos, all Ladinos. They were all intellectuals. In the battles there weren't many Ladinos. We belonged to the Partido Guatemalteco del Trabajo (Guatemalan Communist Party). Our commandant was Cardosa, but he had already been killed.

We come to realize that the indigenous were the majority in the guerrilla and in the army…we were killing each other. Some belonged to one guerrilla group and some to another one with different ideas. So, that's why we decided to call the four commandants to a meeting in Nicaragua. The Frente Sandinista de Liberación Nacional (Sandinista National Liberation Front) gave us access to Nicaragua around October or November '81. The four commandants from the different guerrilla groups got together to discuss the war strategy. In Nicaragua, a group of us Mayas asked the leaders about what the role of the indigenous was going to be, since we knew that we were the majority. In every factory, industry, we were always the workers. The leaders responded by telling us that they'll take care of that after the war. So we said that if a decision is not made before then, the war will be a failure. We told them, "We will continue to fight if you give us an answer now to that question."

"Why?" they asked. We said, "Because we demand justice and you are a minority in all parties." For example, in the battles that I was in there were about 50 to 60 Ladinos, while we Maya were about 500.

Towards the end of '82, we started to get discouraged. We stayed at the battlefront, even though the commanders hadn't answered our petition. And then '82, '83 went by, and at the beginning of '84 the army attacked us with international help. If it had only been the Guatemalan army, we could have won, we had the advantage. But when there was intervention from Chile and the U.S., Argentina, and other countries, we started to lose power. I remember when we were bombarded in March. It lasted for three months, and our strategists had not anticipated all of that. And also after we had that meeting with the commandants, many of our fellows started to give up, since they realized that the power would remain in the hands of the Ladinos.

We crossed the Mexican border without knowing it. In June the Mexican government caught us, and we had no other option but to ask for political asylum there. The Mexicans asked us to hand over our weapons, raise our hands, and identify ourselves. We told them that we would not give up the arms since we were Guatemalan patriots, we were revolutionary soldiers.

'We are going to shoot you,' they said. We told them, 'So, we will all shoot each other here. You die with us.' They asked our leader to come forward. He said, 'Let's talk, we are Guatemalan guerrillas, we are in the middle of an armed fight against the regime, and we didn't realize that we had trespassed into Mexican territory.' We asked to speak to a high army and government authority. After a few days of talks, after the United Nations Commissioner and Amnesty International got there, they asked where we wanted to go. 'Do you want to go back to

Guatemala or do you want political asylum? You can go to
Canada, Italy, Panama. Or do you want to stay in Mexico?' they
asked. I stayed in Mexico.

I had been in Mexico for about a year when I heard the
news about my brothers being caught. There was a newspaper
there, *El Día*. I still have the article from the newspaper. Of
course I felt the need to come back. I couldn't believe it. What
had happened? So I called a friend, a Catholic priest, to ask him.
He told me yes, they'd been kidnapped. I said it couldn't be true,
because I had been making an effort for my brother to leave. I
had spoken with him on the phone and had written him, and
he had told me that they were being persecuted. But I never
thought that Carlos would be the first to go. As I told you at the
beginning, their only fault was to help the people, they didn't
join the armed groups like me.

Definitely, it was very dangerous to consider coming back.
Even in '85, before my brothers were kidnapped, I met a
Guatemalan who was there in Mexico, and he told me not to
go to Guatemala, or not even try to contact my family. He said,
'Every week, every two weeks, the army is patrolling your father's house. They are not uniformed, they dress normal, but
they are around the house because there are rumors that you
will go there, and they may get you. Even the photograph from
your ID card, they have it.' Well, maybe it's because I'm so handsome...

Our leaders told us that we were fighting because we
wanted to create a more just and humane society. In the mountains the men and women guerrillas fought side by side. The relationship was one of mutual respect. They, as well as us, had to
help each other like human beings. Here at home there were
jobs that in the family are specific to the women. There, the

men had to do that job, learn the work of women, and we all did it equally.

The problem here at home is that even the husband puts the wife aside. We see how tiring women's work is: do the laundry, clean, cook, work that is not seen but is exhausting. But in the mountains men and women had to cook, both had to carry their packs and their weapons on their backs. Men or women that were sick were taken care of as human beings. There wasn't that attitude like 'Hey, since you are a woman, bring me that.' No, the men and women were worth the same.

There was one occasion in which a woman was shot in her leg, and couldn't walk. She couldn't take care of her chores in the mountains and even though there were four or five other women, they were far away. So, one of the *compañeros* (comrades) asked us who would be willing to wash her clothes, her underwear, and we all raised our hands. It's a sign of solidarity, that there wasn't any prejudice. But around here we think that if a man helps a woman with laundry, that man is not manly. We wanted that, to achieve equality between women and men. We did not expect to fight just for power in government, but also for liberation, in financial aspects and to improve women's marginal role.

I was with the guerrillas for four-and-a-half years, and then I was in Mexico for eighteen years. Twenty-two years. My wife and children were here in Guatemala, the children went to school, my wife supported them. I only saw them two or three times. I couldn't return until the peace was signed at the end of '96. I finally decided to come back because of my family. When I joined the war, my purpose wasn't just for my family. I wanted a better life for a whole population, a whole republic, a country. I didn't realize how I was endangering my family. I was focused on ideals. I came back, but returned to Mexico because I could not find a way to fit in here.

I wish I could still be in Mexico—I won't deny it—because they gave me a hand. Not only the people who helped me when they found out that I was a Guatemalan guerrilla, that I was politically persecuted, but also because I could get a job. I had work, as much as I wanted. I know how to be a tailor, so I could make a living.

We were trying to create a 'new man'. One day a newspaper reporter asked us whether the new man was like the indigenous, all short and with a big belly. One of our compañeros said, 'No, we are just passing by. The new man and his children are the ones that are going to be born in the future, because we bring too much baggage from the past.'

If I had physical strength, I would join the fight again.

. . . .

The final testimonio was given by Carlos's father. When we first arrived in town we went to meet him and his wife on the roof of their house. Carlos's mother was sitting on the roof sorting red and black beans, her arthritic hands quick and efficient. She nodded when we were introduced, then turned back to her beans. Carlos's son said to his grandfather, "My friend would like to ask questions about your experiences during the violence." The father stared at me. "Are you CIA?" he demanded. "I'll talk to you if you're not CIA." Even ten years after peace was officially declared, a Guatemalan still has to be sure who he's talking to; he still has to determine if it's safe to talk openly.

. . . .

"In 1987 I wrote this and went directly to the Palace. 'Christ died because of the truth...I confront you in God's court. There is justice there...'"
—Carlos's father

CARLOS'S FATHER'S WAR

Carlos's father is 80 years old. We talked in his tailor shop with a rack of elegant men's suits hanging behind him. He and his wife had three sons.

I'm going to tell you just a little because to say a lot I need a very long time. When la violencia started, the army raped the women, all the pretty women. The army cut down the milpa (cornfields). So people got angry. We knew all of that because of the news. It hadn't happened here yet, but we heard it. My son, Carlos, was a rural health nurse who was working in a health center. The guerrillas went to the health center to steal medicines. Then the army came and the mayor told them that he was a guerrilla man, because he let the guerrillas in when they came for help. That's how the army got the wrong information about him. Carlos realized this and left to go work at a farm. But there was a lot of violence in that community too, so he left there to look for work somewhere else. He lived in the capital city. But one day, June 30th, no, June 5th, 1985, he was kidnapped. The kidnappers were from the G2 (military intelligence).

So, for a few days we went looking for him, crying, going all around, but we can't find him. Then, his boss went with us looking for him, too. We found out that he was tortured cruelly for three days even though they said they didn't find that he'd done anything wrong. We were negotiating, but at the last minute they said that it wasn't their choice, they couldn't let go anyone that was intelligent. Otherwise, they might spread the word of what has happened.

We tried for a year, but we got nothing, nothing from the army. And then we learned that he had been at the army quarters in Chimaltenango. That's how we knew he was dead. He disappeared. Was he killed in Chimaltenango? Or is he alive?

We still have hope that he may return one day or he may be dead, we don't know for sure. This is what we have suffered...

For two years we went to the morgue in Guatemala City. There were many corpses there, tortured, but we couldn't find him. A friend of mine, an evangelical, told me he would go look in the book where the army records the names of the dead, I gave him money to look, but he said he didn't find the names of my sons. That's the only information he gave us, and at the end I don't know whether he was telling the truth.

My son-in-law worked at the Co-op Unión Campesina. They assumed that everybody who worked there was a communist. When he was there he started a project to export cauliflower and broccoli. But, since he was in the group with the peasants, they thought they were training him to be a communist or guerrilla. So, the police went after him and he hid. He asked a friend, 'What is it that I'm doing, I'm just working, and why do the police follow me?' So, that person went to the police, and asked them why they were following him since all he's doing is working. So, they left him alone for a while. Then a year later the army came to his home, and he wasn't there, but they chased him and got him. That's his great fault, to be working, and to study law. On July 5, 1985 he was taken. Those were the great wrong-doings that my sons committed.

In 1985 and '86 I left my home here and went to look for them, everywhere, hungry. Then, in 1987, I came home and wrote this: *Christ died because of the truth, but I confront you in God's court. There is justice there, and if my sons are criminals, or you are the criminals, we'll confront you before God's tribunal.* I went directly to the palace in the capital. I said that, and they didn't do anything to me, and here I am alive.

I said, "Mister President, Ministers, Minister of Defense, Army Generals, examine your conscience, because you are the ones that kidnapped my sons, and if you believe in God, you still have time to free them." I pulled out the Holy Bible, "There are those who pretend to be Christians, like General Rios Montt…" So I told them that, and I'm still alive.

My other son realized that the army had been around too much, he decided to flee. I don't know whether it was psychological, or he was also being persecuted. He went to live in another country for twenty years. And that's why he is alive and came back now, about ten years after the peace was made…because when they first signed the peace accords they continued to kill people.

We cried because it was all very sad. I believed that all of my sons were dead. A priest came and we started talking about my sons' kidnappings. 'How many children do you have?' he said. 'Are they all here?' I told him, no, two of my sons and also my son-in-law were kidnapped, but my other son escaped. He asked if I knew whether he was alive or dead. I couldn't say anything for sure.

He pulled out a briefcase, and he said he knew him…He had a letter from my surviving son. 'He is alive?' I didn't know what to do, but I believed it would be better if he doesn't come back here until there is peace. After a few years, we communicated, and I went to look for him, and I found him. I got one son back. About the other two…I don't know anything.

What can I do? That's life. But here in Guatemala we believed that the army should go to the mountains to fight the guerrillas there. They should not attack the people in their homes. I'm angry, too. The mayor was killed here, because the army commander is the one that kills everybody. I'm also on a 'black list' of people to be killed and I pray to God nothing happens. The army here is not human, they are wild beasts. They think that they own Guatemala or life (itself). They don't respect God.

Well, now we don't cry that much during the day, but my wife sometimes says at night, 'Wake up, wake up, why are you crying?' We cry in our sleep. Day and night, always in tears. There are certain songs that Carlos and my other son used to like and one night my wife heard one of them and started crying. I'm sure I won't forget until the day that I die.

Since I'm a Christian, Catholic, the priests always come to see me, to give me fortitude. One day they were going to tell me who the people were who accused my sons of being communists, but I didn't want to know, because it'll just make more trouble. My conscience is at peace. It doesn't matter if I cry day and night.

This is very sad about Guatemala and they don't understand in the US what happened here. More than five hundred years ago the Spaniards killed our people, took our gold and our land. We are poor, and the sons of Spaniards took our farms, and then came back to kill us. It has been said that we, the indigenous, are saints. We are not killers, but if we had weapons now, I'd kill them. We were born good, but with everything that has been done to us, we became rebels because we can't stand it anymore.

Maybe Carlos will show up one day, but…

Jennifer Harbury is a North American activist and lawyer who has written extensively about the guerrilla movement and the Guatemalan civil war. Her hunger strikes in 1994 forced the US government to acknowledge CIA involvement in torture and murder during la violencia. In the following interview, she echoes precisely what Carlos's family said about those who "disappeared."

> …we saw in Latin America, (that torture) ranged
> from church people teaching reading and writing
> or community health care. It went to innocent in-

digenous peasants who were trying to form co-ops....people who were doing health promotion in rural areas. It was anybody trying to end the cycle of poverty in Latin America—unionists, professors, etc. Anybody could be picked up and tortured if the army didn't like them, and the army could substitute itself for the courts of law.

Having a loved one "disappear" and the uncertainty associated with never finding a body have many consequences. Here in one single family, we hear from a young man who was a little boy when his father died; from a wife who lost her husband, the father of her children; from a brother who lost his brothers and returned home only to feel like a stranger in his own country. We hear from a father whose two sons and son-in-law were murdered, who vacillates between believing that they are all dead, and praying that, somehow, miraculously, they will return home. He had the courage and rage to confront government officials, demanding the truth of what had happened to his family. He marvels that he himself is still alive.

8

Women

"My mother was raped. The soldiers who came raped her. And my dad didn't forgive, he didn't understand, and he was very violent to her. My mom said, 'Who can I tell this to, your dad doesn't understand me, many men were inside of me and now what am I going to do? Thank God, that there is no fruit of theirs, but I have such shame. I threw myself on top of all you children when the soldiers came, trying to hide you, wanting them not to discover and kill you. That's the reason for my alcoholism,' my mother said. She felt guilty; she said, 'It was my fault, I should have denied them, better they would have killed me.' But we said, 'Thank God, they didn't kill you because now you are with us. We appreciate you. We love you,' and that's how my mother stopped being an alcoholic."

—anonymous 25-
year-old woman

Ana Clemencia, a 23-year-old university student also talked about rape: "My mother tells me that when she was young—she was 18 then—they were always afraid and I think they still feel it, because she told me that even seeing the army made them afraid. What they did was rape the young women, so my mother would hide so that she wasn't raped." Although Ana Clemencia hadn't even been born yet, she is still a victim: "Even though I didn't live through it, just by knowing so many stories, I feel hurt. And I wonder why these things happened (to us) since we are not animals.

Ana Clemencia

. . . .

Throughout history rape has been used as a weapon of war. This is one reason that women experience war differently than men. And if they are mothers, the safety and welfare of their children is a primary concern. During the violence many women were raped; many mothers suffered trying to protect their children.

In his testimonio, Fernando described his mother's suffering after her husband and son were murdered and she fled to the capital with her eight children. She could not speak Spanish, she had no way to support herself, her traditional clothes identified her as being from the highlands.

"My mother never left (the country), which is another part of the story, too. My uncles and everyone, they think to help the men, but no one thought of my mother with her children. The ones who were alone, those with fewer children, they could run away, but my mother was a woman with eight children, no one ever worried about her. She was practically abandoned—her bad luck—here in the capital."

Violence altered every aspect of women's lives, often requiring that they make changes in their traditional roles, as we can see from the testimonio of the mother who was raped, and from the experiences of Fernando's mother. Lykes explains:

> Although many women were killed and/or disappeared, they were more likely than men to survive, facing the burden of the psychosocial and material consequences of this violence. Among their many responses to the violence, it is important to note their multiple contributions to the maintenance and growth of families and communities. This can be seen not only in the many new roles that women have increasingly occupied in rural communities (e.g. tending large animals, preparing fields for planting, chopping wood, participating in local religious and political organizations) but also in the leadership positions in human rights organizations that they have assumed.

The *REHMI Report* provides another perspective regarding the vital role that women played in searching for the truth about what happened to family members.

> The search for relatives who have been disappeared has been one of the most anguishing struggles arising from political repression, and one that has been spearheaded by women...In the face of such dire circumstances, women have displayed an enormous capacity to avoid becoming discouraged, to pull themselves together, and to undertake new stategies...The search became the only means of standing up to the army and defying the terror.

"I heard in the Quiché the great suffering that had happened to the people. A woman named Dona Micaela told me about when the army tortured and killed the men in her community. They killed seven members of her family. She said, 'I don't have any more tears to cry. I have cried so much for my relatives, for my loved ones. Now I don't have any more tears.'"

—Laura

LAURA'S WAR

Laura is the young woman who feels it is her "mission" to help survivors tell their stories. She takes testimonios, and accompanies family members to mass graves where bodies are being exhumed. While she says that the violence did not directly affect her or her family, she experiences a kind of vicarious post-traumatic stress having heard and absorbed so much tragedy from the people she counsels. In this part of her testimonio, she talks about the many mothers who struggled against impossible odds to protect their children.

Laura

Laura is a 28-year-old K'iche' Maya woman who works as a mental health worker in rural communities where she conducts support groups for victims of the violence.

One story that is always with me is a woman who told me, 'It's Rios Montt's fault that I killed my son. I am a murderer!' Because she was pregnant when they had to escape to the mountains. The baby was born in the mountains...it's normal for a baby to cry a lot. But the group she was with told her, 'Quiet that baby! They are going to hear us. You have to quiet him!' So she covered his mouth and nose. The baby got sick. He didn't die right away, he died five days later. She remembers this all the time. She says, 'I am a murderer. I killed my son. If I hadn't killed him, he would be twenty years old.'

Hearing these stories, trying to tell her she is not a murderer, that it's not her fault, is very difficult. Because when the people have suffered a lot, they see everything in black and white. They can only see the black and not the strengths that they have. It's like that for this mother who survived, and was able to take care of her smaller children after she became a widow. She was left with four little children, and the fact that she managed to take care of them means that she is a strong woman. But she isn't able to see that light in her life.

Another mental health worker said:

One lady told me, 'I am going to take this with me to the grave, I am going to die with this, with my pain.' She counts how old her child who died would be. Others grieve over the deaths of grandparents, or great-grandparents who died when they were not that old.

Carlos, a 23-year-old law student, described the atrocities that were perpetrated against the women in his village. "When all the women got to the center of the town they grabbed the babies out of the arms of their mothers—because in our town they didn't kill children. They took them out of their mothers' arms and they gave the children away. Today I know three girls—well, now they are women—that this happened to. They were given away, my father says he thinks that it was the captain of the army who did it. He called out to all the neighbors, to the women who wanted babies, and he gave them away."

Antonio is an engineering student who said he didn't feel the need to talk: "Nothing bad happened in my family so I don't have anything to say." But after listening quietly to the other testimonios, he told this story:

> One of my uncles, my mother's brother, had just finished his teaching degree and was working in a community in the Ixcán. At that time transportation was very limited and he had to walk for a couple of days to get to his job, he would stay there a long time—a month, two months—and he would come home for a week or two. My mother tells me that during his last trip he came to see her, and that was the last time they heard about him. They don't know anything else. We don't know how, or when (he died), and I think that left a mark forever, mainly in my grandmother, his mother.

Here we have women survivors of the Guatemalan civil war: women raped and then shunned by their husbands, women desperately trying to protect their children; women calling themselves guilty because they could not "prevent" themselves from being raped. Here we have mothers traumatized trying to save their children, calling themselves "murderers" because their children died. Here are women grieving for their children who never returned home.

Are there life-long repercussions of the violence these women experienced? Certainly it occurred many years before and they are urged, overtly and covertly, to "get on" with their lives. But what are the far-reaching consequences of being a victim, yet calling yourself a murderer? of losing a beloved child and not being able to give him or her a proper burial? Are these effects still felt in Guatemalan society today. Are the consequences passed on to the next generation?

After reading this chapter, a Guatemalan human rights activist wrote, "This is a very valuable testimony. There has been very little reflection on the dramatic increase in alcoholism among women, or of the increase in violence against women in Guatemala today which are direct consequences of the war."

· · · · · ·

I am sitting across the table from a young woman who was nine years old when she watched her father being was taken away. Now thirty-three, she has a seven-year-old son. She starts talking in a matter-of-fact way about the morning her father was dragged off. She is in that moment; she starts to shake. It's clear that she's no longer here in this sunny courtyard sitting together with her husband and two young children. She's become that little girl saying goodbye to her papa, afraid that she'll never see him again, even though he calls to her, "Don't worry, daughter, I will be home tonight."

She starts to cry. Her little boy, José, glances over, and then, eyes wide, he leans into her.

"Has anything helped?" I ask, helpless.

"Yes," she catches her breath. "It helped for the first time when I had him," pulling her son close. He buries his face in her chest; they sit folded into each other, quieting one another.

9
Lost Children

MANY CHILDREN SURVIVED, IN SPITE OF BEING LOST, or displaced, or abandoned. Perhaps every person who survives genocide should be considered a "lost child". These stories, one written by Eliseo, and those told by Víctoria and her husband, Ical, speak most poignantly about the loss of a parent and the lifelong trauma that is its consequence.

In their study of the effect of terrorism on Maya children, Melville and Lykes state: "Nowhere do children face more deplorable situations nor more physical and psychological aggression than during wartime." They review research which shows that children who remain close to a parent or loving caretaker experience less severe trauma. And they document the importance of giving children an explanation of their reality, to help them try to make sense of their world. The *REHMI Report* supports this:

> Children need to understand what happened to them and to their families. When their search for meaning is met with lack of communication, silence, or contradictory explanations from adults, the impact of violence may be exacerbated...clear explanations...together with efforts to preserve the

memory of their family members, can help them reconstruct their sense of identity.

During the initial meeting in March, Eliseo was the only student who did not give a testimonio. Afterwards I found him leaning against a wall, crying. "Laurie, I am so sorry I could not speak."

"Eliseo," I said, "you don't have to speak, you can just listen. Or you can write your story. It's like a poison inside, you can help yourself heal by writing the story out."

At 5'6", Eliseo is tall for a Maya man. He bent down, resting his head on my shoulder. Then, straightening up, "Thank you," he said. "I will."

When I left a week later Eliseo handed me a manila envelope, taped and double-stapled. Across the top he had written in capital letters, "Please do not open this until you get to the United States. Do not open this in Guatemala."

In *Trauma and Recovery*, Judith Herman reminds us :

> Trauma inevitably brings loss. Even those who are lucky enough to escape physically unscathed still lose the internal psychological structures of a self securely attached to others...those who lose important people in their lives face a new void in their relationships with friends, family, or community.

She goes on to discuss the importance of telling what she calls the "trauma story," describing the manner in which trauma survivors recount experiences:

> People who have survived atrocities often tell their stories in a highly emotional, contradictory, and fragmented manner which undermines their credibility and thereby serves the twin imperatives of truth-telling and secrecy."

And Mersky offers this definition of testimony: "...memory of the lived experience, told freely...(it) is not necessarily all of what is remembered, nor all of what happened; rather it is what the person can or wants to tell us at that moment."

Here, Eliseo's story is told in its entirety, exactly as written, with the intent of, as Mersky says, "respect[ing] the testimony as a whole, and thus the integrity of the experience."

. . . .

> I'm a victim that has maintained his story in silence, and I write it now hoping that those who read it believe all of it, please.
>
> —Eliseo

ELISEO'S WAR

Eliseo is a 27-year-old Kaqchikel Maya man completing dual degrees in accounting and law at the University of San Carlos. At times, Eliseo's words practically scream from the page: "Believe this, it is my story."

I hope you understand the spirit of what I wrote, I hope it will be translated word for word, so that it won't change the sentiment. Sorry if there is any mistake or some words crossed out, but each time I wrote, I became very nervous. If there's anything you don't understand, please ask me about it. I noticed that it feels very good to write about my past. I would like to write my story more technically, more orderly, so that it can be understood better, maybe someday I will be able to do it. Thanks for listening and reading my story.

In this moment, I prepare myself to write my story, I try to remember everything possible, I'm going to try to write all that I remember and all that they have told me, it's my own story—very sad, but my own. It's a story that never has been told or listened to in its entirety, no one has ever interviewed me. I'm a victim that has maintained his story in silence, and I write it now hoping that those who read it believe all of it, please. I will not write any lie here, and I hope that the translation will be the most accurate possible so that it won't confuse what I am trying to tell you.

It makes me very sad to remember that I was only five years old, when these wretched men took away from me what I most loved—they took away my father and my mother. We lived in a very humble house in the village of Pamumús (which in Spanish, means place of rainy weather). This village belongs to the municipality of San Juan Comalapa, in the department of Chimaltenango. It was a very humble village. To get to it, you had to walk a lot of time through the mountains. I remember that you had to cross a river where I used to love to play. My life for those first five years was normal. I played, laughed, cried, always had my parents and siblings near me. In my house we had chickens that gave us many eggs, pigs, some cows, and a dog that I played with (we had to leave all the little animals). Then, what I remember is that one day they all left, and I was left only with my sister Luisa—they didn't tell me where they went. What I remember is that that day they did not return. My family didn't come back until the following day, but when they did, not everyone that had left returned. We never again saw my mother nor one uncle.

When I grew up, they told me that when they left me in the house with Luisa, they had gone to the graduation of my older sister, Patricia. My sister was going to receive her degree as a teacher in primary education. She studied in the nuns' boarding school called the Indigenous Institute of Our Lady of Mercy, in Guatemala City. And due to the distance, they hadn't been able to return to the village, so they stayed at my uncle's

house. Then, the next day, they started walking towards Pamumús, and as they went walking, some men blocked off their
path, and without explanation, they took my mother and one
uncle. Then they told my siblings and other family members
that they should go quickly, without turning around to look,
because if they didn't, the men would kill them. They had to
obey the orders of the damned soldiers because they were afraid
of being killed, except my brother Pedro, who very bravely told
them that they should take him instead of my mother, but they
hit him and told him brusquely, 'No.' I don't know if they took
anyone else. We never again saw my mother. My uncle emigrated, first to the Petén, and then to Mexico, because they were
chasing him to kill him.

It's not easy to remember and write this. Because when one
graduates, it's a reason to be happy and have parties, these
tragedies turned off our happiness. I think of how my sister must
have felt in this moment—no one could explain why they had
taken my little mother, nobody could give us an explication.
But the nastiness of these people didn't end there. I remember,
some time had passed, (I don't remember exactly how long it
was). One night, when my mother was no longer with us, they
knocked on the door. We were very scared. We lived with a lot
of fear ever since they kidnapped my mommy. I remember that
one of my brothers opened the door and a man asked for my
father. My father came out to see what was going on (note that
my father was one of the leaders of the village of Pamumús. He
was a very active man, he liked to work for the family and for
the village. He had a very strong character, and we had to obey
him or he would punish us.) My father spoke for a good
amount of time with the men, and afterwards, he spoke with my
older brothers and then he went out into the darkness. Like always, they didn't tell me anything of what was happening.

(When I was old enough, they told me that my father had to leave in a hurry because people were searching for him to kill him, and these men that had come knocking on the door had been sent by the military to kill him. But instead they just told him to disappear to make it look like he had been killed, and there was no other way but for him to escape and leave us to ourselves.)

I try to remember with accuracy how much longer we stayed in the village of Pamumús, but it's not possible. The only thing I remember is that later, we left, walking in the mountains, but it wasn't where we always walked, because I remembered well the path that went to San Juan Comalapa (since then I haven't returned to Pamumús, my siblings have, but I could not return to this place. If I return, it could end up that I remember many things that would make me even more sad). We walked for a long time, carrying the least necessities possible.

Then we arrived at San Juan Comalapa, and we stayed the night in my uncle's house. The next day, my siblings decided to travel to Antigua, Guatemala, since the School of Our Lady of Mercy had relocated to Antigua, and I stayed with my brother Pedro for some time in my uncle's house. My uncle loved me very much—I remember that he bought me a pair of shoes, because I didn't use to wear shoes very much in the village where we lived. But these shoes that he bought me hurt me, because I wasn't used to wearing shoes. My sister Luisa stayed with my grandmother, she loved her very much, but Luisa didn't feel good there and, for this reason, she didn't stay there very long. Then one day my brother Pedro decided that we would go to look for my other siblings. We wanted to be together, so that was how we ended up traveling to Antigua to look for the School of Our Lady of Mercy. When we found my siblings, they had missed seeing us, but we couldn't all be in this boarding school because it was only for girls. My sister Patricia spoke with the nun that was the director, to see if we could stay there for some time. The director accepted that we would stay for a while. The director helped my sister Patricia find a place where we would all be able to stay, and it was like this that we traveled to the capital and the director brought us to a boarding school called Hogar del Niño (Home of the Boy), that was directed by Italian nuns that took in orphaned boys. So my siblings just left me there. I remember that when they left me they told me they were going to come back, and that they were only going to buy an ice cream. I asked about my parents, of course, I didn't know what had happened to them, and I cried and cried and cried until I didn't have the strength to cry. I remember that it was very hard on me, because I couldn't speak Spanish. I could only speak Kaqchikel and this school was mostly taught by Italian and Colombian nuns, and none of the boys spoke my language either. I remember that I failed the first year in the school, but in this year I learned to speak a bit of Spanish, and the next year I repeated the first year of school and had a Colombian teacher. She was a very good person, like my mother. She even wanted to bring me to her country, but I didn't want to go because I wanted to be with my siblings, even though I rarely saw them.

Meanwhile, the director of the School of Our Lady of Mercy looked for a place where the rest of my siblings could stay, my two brothers—Pedro and Jorge—stayed in the Indigenous Institute of Santiago which was another boarding school for indigenous boys. What made me the most sad though, was what happened with my youngest sister, Laura. At that time, she was three years old, meaning that at the time my parents disappeared, she was only two years old, and it was she that most needed my mother's care, she was only a little baby. They found a place called Mather Orphanage in Guatemala City that was directed by nuns. It was hard for them (my sisters) to get accepted to this school given that Laura was very small and needed special care. And Natalia, my other sister, wore the indigenous clothing of San Juan Comalapa, and she didn't want to take it off. Only by much insisting did they get permission for the girls to stay at this boarding school. What they told me afterwards was that my sister Laura was close to dying because she was so tiny and the treatment and food wasn't adapted for her and only thanks to God, did she survive. My sister Natalia stayed in this boarding school until she graduated as a skilled accountant, and my little sister Laura, she was only there until sixth grade, since Natalia had graduated and she didn't want to be there alone. Natalia started studying in the University of San Carlos of Guatemala, but she couldn't finish. Laura graduated from the School of Our Lady of Mercy as a teacher of primary education, and then began law studies in the University of San Carlos of Guatemala but because of problems, she couldn't finish. Maybe some day my sisters can continue studying in the university.

My sister Luisa stayed in the School of Our Lady of Mercy until she graduated as a teacher of primary education. Then she continued with her studies in the University Rafael Landívar with a scholarship, and now she's actually licensed in bilingual intercultural education.

All of us had different experiences in each school that we were at, but I want to refer to the Hogar del Niño where I ended up staying. I was there for six long years. I say six long years because they were not the best years. In the first year I missed my parents very much and I missed my siblings, since they visited me very little and I became very sad and cried a lot. The nuns that cared for me couldn't understand this, given that they had to care for many more boys and couldn't care only for me. Moreover, they never told me why we didn't go back to the village of Pamumús (though it was very humble, we were happy there), why we weren't with our parents anymore.

I spent many sad moments, for instance, when the rest of the children's families visited and when they were allowed outings to go to their homes, but nobody visited me and I didn't have anywhere to go.

I remember especially when I was about ten years old. They brought us to the doctor in the middle of the city—certain ones of us that had problems with our eyes—and on this occasion, we traveled by bus and the nun came with us to care for us, and I was so excited looking at the buildings, the cars, so many people, so many stores, that I didn't notice when the other kids got off the bus with the nun. I was lost in the city, in a city where I had never been. I cried a lot, I didn't know what to do. I walked for hours in the streets, until a policeman asked me, 'Why are you crying?' And I answered that I was lost and that I studied in the school Hogar del Niño. The police gave me one quetzal and left me on a bus, telling the driver that he should leave me at the Hogar del Niño. I rode alongside the driver, but surprise! he told me that we had arrived, and showed that here was the Hogar del Niño. I began to cry and I told him that this wasn't the Hogar del Niño. The driver gave me some food, since it was already lunch time, and I had no idea where I was. The bus had gone the whole length of the city, and then the driver continued his route and gave me directions that I should get off in the place that he would show me and that there, I would board another bus that had the number 10 on it (what luck that I could read and write). And that's how I did it. When I got on the bus with the number 10, I felt more lost, since I didn't know where it was going to stop, but I sat down next to the driver and told him that I wanted to arrive at the Hogar del Niño that was in Zone 7. He told that yes, he knew of the place. The bus took a

long time to get to Zone 7 and every minute that passed, I got
more scared, since I didn't know the places that the bus was
passing. I felt happy when I saw a market that at the time was
called La Samaritana (actually it was called 'La Económica,' but
it didn't have any economy) and quickly I signaled the driver
that I would get off here. Once I got off, I didn't know what to
do, I was very afraid of what the nuns were going to say to me.
I walked and walked each step with more fear and urges to cry.
At one point, I thought it was better to just stay lost, when all
of a sudden I saw my brother, Pedro. I called him and told him
what had happened, but before I could tell him everything, I
had already started crying bitterly. He calmed me and brought
me to the Hogar del Niño. The nuns were very happy to see me,
because I had come back. They hugged me and told me that
most of the nuns had gone out to look for me. They asked me
to tell them how I got back on my own, but I couldn't even tell
them because I was crying so much. In that moment, I knew
that there did exist people that worried about me, but it wasn't
enough. I wanted the love of my parents and my siblings.

This is only one of the things that happened to me, all of
my siblings had different experiences. My sister Patricia could
not care for six siblings. She started to work as a teacher in primary education, in a village in the municipality of Sumpango.
Patricia had to walk a lot to get to the village, and she earned
80 quetzales (about $10) each month, which wasn't even
enough to support her, much less support her six siblings.

We had many sorrows of all types. Another of the things
that at the moment didn't seem very important because I was a
small boy that had just barely started to understand the world,
was when I started to travel alone to Antigua, one day my
brother Jorge arrived to visit me, but only to tell me that I
shouldn't come to Antigua for a while because my sister Patri-

cia had had her baby die, and no one was free to take care of me. I was left thinking a lot about why I had never had the opportunity to see my sister pregnant, and how she almost never visited us, and now even less since the loss of my nephew. It's very painful to describe all of this, because at this time, I suffered from a lot of things that a normal boy wouldn't have to suffer, and since this moment, I never again asked for my parents.

I studied six years in the Hogar del Niño, and then I studied in a different boarding school of Italian priests, called the vocational center of San José, and I studied there for three years. In this school, I had to skip the last year due to the fact that I didn't want to be closed in anymore.

This next part of my story that follows is the part that very few know. Maybe it is the saddest because it was when I was older and could understand more about things, and on one occasion, my brothers Pedro and Jorge (they were studying in their final year in order to graduate as primary school teachers) brought me to the municipality of Sumpango, to a place where a man lived. My brothers were doing their work in Sumpango, and they lived with this man, and I also stayed with him once in a while. This man had a very kind wife and they also had a son. For much time we had many interactions with this family, but I asked myself, who would this man be? I never asked anyone else, just like I didn't ask anything about what had happened to us in the past, and nobody told me about it. (Now I understand why they didn't tell me about it.)

Little by little my siblings started to tell me some things, and what they told me caused me much sadness, and I couldn't believe them. One day, talking with a friend of my siblings, he told me something that I do not forget. This friend told me the man we had been going to visit in Sumpango was my father. I was dumbfounded and didn't know how to answer him, because my siblings had told me that the soldiers had kidnapped and killed my mother and father. I didn't tell my siblings what this friend had told me, until one day I told my brother, Jorge. He answered me that it wasn't true, and that I shouldn't believe the friend because he was joking. (The truth was that they didn't want me to know, because then I might tell about it if the soldiers asked us). So I believed my brother more than the friend, because the man that was supposedly my father lived with his wife and son, so it was impossible that he be my father.

Three years passed, (in which my sisters Natalia and Luisa graduated as accountant and teacher, respectively) and during that time, I had the opportunity to go back to the man in Sumpango (I mention this man a lot, but I never knew his name, they only told me that he was a friend). He missed me a lot. The fact was that we always found this man living in a different place. We never found him in the same house, he changed houses constantly, but, well, when I returned to see him this time, he lived out in the fields, very far away from the center of the village. In fact, all the houses that he had lived in had the characteristic of being very far from the village. We always had to walk far, and this time it was very far from the village. The man let us into his humble house and, as usual, he offered us something to eat or to drink. My brother, Pedro spoke for a good while with him in private and then the man gave us a box of tomatoes and other vegetables. We said goodbye, and we left. We were waiting for the bus when in one moment, Pedro broke the silence that had invaded to tell me the following: 'This man that we come to visit so much is our father.'

(For whoever is reading these lines, I want them to know that in this moment, I spill some tears, I take a rest in order to be able to return to writing. It's not easy for me to tell about this, I would like to overcome this, but it is very hard for me.

Perhaps some day I will be able to overcome it.)

I stayed completely quiet, because after 10 years, my father ended up to be this man that I had known for about 5 years. I asked myself the following questions: Why doesn't he live with us? Why did he abandon us? Why didn't they tell me this when I first met him?

I didn't know what to say, I took this good man as a person that wanted to help us. (In the course of my life, there have been many people that have extended their hand to us to help us for no reason). I stayed absolutely quiet, I didn't know what to say, I didn't know what to do, I didn't know whether to start crying or leave running and hug him for the reuniting. But no, I didn't do anything, nor did I say anything. Pedro didn't say anything else to me, he just told me that they hadn't told me before because I was too young, and that I wouldn't understand. I didn't protest at all, I didn't say anything, I was completely confused. I never told anyone this, I didn't have anyone I could trust that I could tell. During the nights, I thought a lot and cried a lot, I asked myself thousands of questions, like the following: why didn't my father look for us earlier so that we could be together? Why does my father have another wife and, at that moment, he had three kids with the other wife? Was it possible that my mother also was alive and we just didn't know where she was? I asked myself thousands of questions, but I didn't ask them of anyone else. I swallowed everything alone. I lived and continue living always pensive, sad, timid, swallowing all of my problems. I ask my brothers very few things, but when we all get together, sometimes they start to tell about things that happened to us and I take advantage of this to learn about more things from my past, from our past.

I asked myself why my father looked to have another family, and I asked myself if my mother was maybe alive in some place in Guatemala or Mexico. It hurt me a lot that it was hard for me, but it was hard for me to say 'dad' to this man, since I had already known him, and had never called him dad. Moreover, I didn't like that he had another family, because if he didn't have the other family, he would have been able to live with us. During the trip home, nobody said anything, we all were very pensive. I thought and asked myself, 'When are we going to see him again?' so that I could have the opportunity to ask the questions that I had always wanted to ask him.

The only person that knows more or less all of this is the woman Lucía, because after the re-meeting, I told her everything. She is the only person that has known how to listen to me. She has given me breath to keep moving forward. I told her how I didn't feel comfortable calling him 'dad,' but that I respected him a lot. (I'm very grateful to Lucía for listening to me and understanding my tears.)

In Guatemala, we celebrate the 17 of June, the Day of the Father. On one occasion, I went to look for my father in the department of Chimaltenango. It was very hard, and I walked a lot, his house was very far away, but in the end I found him. When I arrived, I found his wife and her kids, I entered the very humble house, and they offered me something to drink. Then I asked them about my father, and they told me that he had gone to work out in the fields (I was very sad because it was the Day of the Father and I thought that he didn't know it.) I asked them where he was working and I went to look for him. I remember that I walked a lot, and I found him picking the crops. Since the crops were very small it was easy to see him. It affected me a lot to see him work, because when I found him, I saw him thoroughly, and I saw him working with a hoe. He worked very slowly. I slowly got closer, until he noticed I was there.

I greeted him, but I couldn't say Happy Father's Day! I don't know why I didn't say it, I spoke to him and asked him if he could give me a little time to talk with him. He told me that only if it would just be a moment, because the owner of the land didn't want him to be resting. The only thing I said was that I wanted to know my story, our story. He began telling me the following:

In San Juan Comalapa, there are some very bad people. (My father told me the names of these people that are actually alive, but I couldn't remember their names.) Some of these people were in love with my mother but since my father married her, they resented my parents. It was so much resentment that these bad people told the soldiers of the government of Rios Montt that my parents were guerrillas and that my sister Patricia was studying with the money that the guerrillas were giving her. It was for this reason that the soldiers had kidnapped my mother. After that some men sent by the army looked for my father to kill him, but thank God these men were not as bad, and they told him that they had been ordered to kill him, but that they knew him and that they knew he didn't have anything to do with the guerrillas. They gave him the opportunity to go very far away so nothing more was ever known of him, and they went to inform the army that they had killed him and hidden the body. So that was how that same night he left the house and traveled to Escuintla. Sadly, at this time, the soldiers found out about everything, and they found out that my father was in a farm in Escuintla, and that was why he traveled to the Petén. He lived there for quite a while, and for all this time he didn't know anything of our existence. He knew where we were living, but the soldiers also knew, and they were watching us to see if he would come to us. Afterwards, he made the trip to Sumpango, and that was when my siblings were close to him, but he was already living with another woman and had one child with her

(he told me many things that he saw and lived when he was in the Petén, he saw many massacres, and this affected me a lot. Thank God that he was still alive and we were, too.)

My next question was, 'And my mother? What happened to my mother? Is she alive?' He told me that he found out that the soldiers had killed her and buried her in a clandestine cemetery that was in a military camp in San Juan Comalapa.

I said goodbye with much sadness, and I was very angry with the stupidity of the men who had assumed that my parents were involved with the guerrillas. My parents were humble workers, they didn't know anything about communism, and for this stupidity, the men changed the destiny of our lives.

Actually in the secret cemetery located in San Juan Comalapa, they are doing exhumations and they have found more than one hundred corpses of people that had been buried in this place. When I went for the first time to this place, I felt very moved to see it. In a pit where some anthropologists were working on the corpses of a group of people that looked like they had been buried alive, and that was what the anthropologists commented. In another pit you could see remains of people that had had the so-called 'shot of grace', others were mutilated with the head between their legs. I don't want to keep mentioning them because the only thing that came to my head was, how did my little mother die? To be able to find the remains of my mother, I had to know how she was dressed the last time we saw her, and the only person who remembered, more or less, was my sister Patricia. We traveled to this place various times with the hope that we would find the remains of my mother. We are sure that her remains would be found in this cemetery because one soldier that was in this place at the time knew my mother and he told us that she had been assassinated there.

I felt very sad when one friend from San Juan Comalapa

told me that they had found a giant oven and that one soldier had given testimony that in this giant oven, they burned the people and that all that was left were their ashes. Then I didn't want to know anymore, because I associated everything with the death of my mother. *

This is what has me so sad. Why, for some stupid reason, did they kill my mother? For some stupidity they disintegrated my family. For some stupidity I lost my language, I lost my culture, we lost our property, because never again did we return to our village. In the end, we lost everything. In reality, it's for my mother that I cry. She didn't have to suffer this. I don't know in what way she died. These people did not have the right to take away the life of my saint mother. She didn't deserve it.

Sweet, darling mother, wherever you are, I want to tell you that I love you very much and I will never forget you. You know very well that someone will do you justice, I love you so much!

But, thank God, that with all our limitations, all our suffering, and thanks to all the people very far from our family that helped us come out ahead. Thanks to the Maya Educational Foundation that granted me a scholarship, that when I graduate, I have to reimburse, but I think that all is possible.

I hope to graduate as a lawyer and notary in December of 2005, and work for the people with few resources. Because I have been thinking that when we, in some moment in our lives needed help, we didn't get it because we have scarce resources.

I would like for peace, tranquility, justice and love to reign

---

* "In the Mayan culture, the dead are considered part of the community and possessors of another form of life. For this reason, exhumations are, for many people, a possibility of reestablishing in part these ties that were broken by violence. For all Ladinos or Mayans, to know what happened to their loved ones and to have a place to go to see them is associated with the closure of the process of hurt." (*REHMI Report*)

in Guatemala. I would like all Guatemalans to be equal, and for there to be no discrimination on grounds of race, culture, religion, ethnicity, and ways of thinking. All of this influenced me to study the career of law, because now that I'm in the situation I'm in, I couldn't study the career that I truly wanted to study, which was architecture. I couldn't because of the time that the career requires and for the expenses associated with it. I worked on the weekends, from Friday nights, Saturday, and Sunday all day and, if necessary, I work sometimes during the week, but I am happy in my career, because I can help many people.

I'm very content, because I'm forming a relationship with my girlfriend, Ana, she's waiting for a precious baby. And I will be a responsible father, I don't want my child to miss the affection of a father, I want my child to be a good person, and when my child grows up, I will tell him of my past so that he can reflect and appreciate life and learn how to respect the rights of everyone in the world. I'm very happy with Ana, because she understands me. She is with me through the good and the bad, she's hardworking, and I know that she will be a good mother. I love her very much.

I hope that you understand what I have written. I tried to write as coherently as possible, I think that I wrote some things that maybe for some (people) aren't important, and also some things I have left out. Maybe it is because I forget in the moment, or because maybe someone in that moment would think I was exaggerating. Of course this isn't my whole story, but if there are any questions over some part that isn't quite clear, you can ask me about it however you want. I don't want you to feel embarrassed to ask. This will help me remember things that I've forgotten.

Finally, I want to thank you for your humanity and solidarity that you have shown towards the Maya people. I want to thank you for being interested in my life and those of my friends, and like I mentioned in the beginning, no one has ever been interested in my past, in my story. This is the first time that I write my story. Sometimes, someone that hasn't lived this will think that I'm exaggerating.

I hope you understand me, really understand, since in one moment, I felt that I was in control of what I felt. I felt that I would tell my story with ease and calm, but it's not like that. (At the group meeting on) the 11th of March, 2005, at 3:00 in the afternoon, I noticed that I hadn't overcome my feelings. On listening to each story of my companions, I felt very affected and when it was my turn, I felt that I had a knot in my throat and I couldn't speak. Since then I have been very sad, remembering many things, there are moments when I am alone that I start crying. When I walk to the library, people have seen me crying, and at night I cry regularly. It gives me sorrow to tell this, but someone will think that I exaggerate. The truth is that only the one that has lived these injustices feels it and understands it.

I want to tell you that I cry for the death of my mother, the way that she died, the reason for her death (it's a stupid, senseless reason). I cry because I can't give her a Christian burial and that there isn't a place where I can leave her a bouquet of roses. In conclusion, *I cry for the death of my mother.*

Thanks for being my friends, for listening to me and understanding my past. This is what happened to me and I don't wish it on anyone else.

Eliseo was scheduled to graduate with his law degree in April, 2006. I knew I couldn't go; it wasn't really my place, anyway. But after reading Eliseo's testimonio—somehow—in spite of how unrealistic it might be, I knew I *had* to be there. So, the day before the graduation I flew to Guatemala City and the next morning a couple of the other students and I drove together to the university. No one, except me, seemed particularly worried about whether we would arrive on time, and, in fact, as we walked in, Eliseo was already standing at the podium reading the dedication to his thesis: "*A mi madre, María, que El Señor la tenga a su diestra y por ensenarme las palabras, Si se puede! Teniendola siempre en mi mente y mi corazon.*" ("To my mother, María, that the Lord has seated at His right hand. It was she who taught me the words 'Yes, you can!' I will always hold her in my mind and my heart.")

As I stood there I realized that, finally, after a lifetime of grief, this is the bouquet of roses he has brought for his mother.

. . . .

In the testimonio we have just read, Eliseo's longing for his mother is palpable. Grief permeates his life; it is never-ending.

In the following testimonios, Víctoria and her husband Ical, also speak of being children of war, of yearning to know what happened to a parent. They feel compelled to search to find, and to re-bury, their bones.

. . . .

"At an early age, the children became little adults; they were no longer able to satisfy their need as children to play or expect the support of their parents."

—Víctoria

VICTORIA'S WAR

Víctoria tells how her father was kidnapped in broad daylight in front of an entire busload of witnesses. His disappearance devastated her family, plunging them into poverty and despair. Víctoria is a 33-year-old Kaqchikel Maya woman who is married and has two children. She has an undergraduate degree in sociology and a graduate degree in communications and works for an organization that monitors media coverage of Maya women.

At about 3:30 on the 13th of September 1981, as my father was walking towards the central square of the village to get on the bus, he was stopped by two men. Without saying a word, they began to beat him, but he was still able to escape and to take shelter in a neighbor's house. She offered him help, but the bus began to leave and he thought that if he got on it, the killers would leave him in peace.

When he got on the bus, he was already bruised and beaten, but the killers also boarded the bus, one in front and another in back. (These men) ordered the driver to stop and they sent for the soldiers to force him off the bus. According to witnesses, he did not want to go, but they hit him and made him. Those who saw it recounted that they dragged him up the hill, and that he was bleeding and they kept hitting him.

The driver still insisted that my father was innocent, but the soldiers threatened all the passengers, saying that they would kill them all immediately if they opposed them.

When my father was captured, he had a document from the Ministry of Defense vouching that he was a citizen and not an enemy or a guerrilla fighter. However, this did not stop them from kidnapping him in front of so many witnesses who saw everything. Since then it has never been determined where they left his remains.

The loss of my father and of our house and everything in it was a traumatic event for me and my siblings who were all very young. After our father was kidnapped our economic situation got worse, because there was no work for children, nor for our mother who couldn't speak Spanish and was illiterate. This meant that we suffered subhuman conditions trying to survive. We did not have housing, we had to live in hallways, we had to beg in order to make it through the day. Even family members did not want to support us, and they tried to make the children work in demeaning conditions of slavery.

Given this state of affairs, our education did not enter into the picture because all of us had to work, except the youngest. So none of us had a chance to study to improve our situation. Even at that young age, the children became little adults. We were no longer able to satisfy our need as children to play or expect the support to our parents. Each one was expected to bring something to eat and to pay for the rent of the hallway where we slept.

We also suffered because the culture of our community in the countryside and the way people interact in the city were different, and this caused much suspicion, fear, apprehension, and a sense of psychological dislocation. My mother, my sisters, and I all had to endure sexual harassment from acquaintances and police officers.

The historical account of all that happened must occur to bring social justice and mental health to the people affected by this period of violence. This has not happened and the effects continue and are, in fact, still felt in the younger generations.

In her writing and interviews, Marcie Mersky speaks about the need to break silence, emphasizing the importance of the exhumations in bringing back the voices of the dead in a different form:

> One of the things that these projects documenting human rights violations have sought to do is to break the silence around these events…the perpetrators felt that by having mass raids and trying to hide the bodies, they could hide the voices as well—that those voices would be buried along with the people who were killed in the massacres.

· · · · · · · ·

"My wife and I went to the exhumation to see if
we can find her father, because my wife can't leave
it alone. It's something she needs to do, she wants
to find her father, where he is, and see it, even if he
is in his bones."

—Ical

ICAL'S WAR

Ical is Víctoria's husband. He tells the story of Víctoria's father
kidnapping, describing her grief and need to find her father, even if
he is "in his bones." Ical is a 32-year-old Q'eqchi Maya man with a
degree in political science from the University of San Carlos.

My father-in-law disappeared in '81, exactly on September
13th, when my wife was 8 years old. He and his family lived in
Comalapa, one of the most affected places. Some military people took him and still, his remains haven't been found. (No one
knows) where he was, where he was killed, and what happened
to him. I'm telling you this because there are going to be consequences for a long time. My wife suffers from nervous break-
downs. She saw what happened: the army took the school, and
in front of the playground where the boys and girls played bas-
ketball, they laid the dead, so that in the town people would
see how the people who they called guerrillas were killed. They
called called it 'exemplary massacres'; this was part of the psychological war.

My wife tells me that she saw how those people were laid
there as if they were chickens, in the sun, already killed. She has
terrible insomnia, and we have to treat her for it constantly. Her
mother has diabetes and high blood pressure which was caused
by that situation. Family relationships have been disrupted, almost destroyed. For example, my wife and her family never

went back to Comalapa, because their own grandparents didn't want to acknowledge them. They accused them of being guerrillas, and for 15 years, they never went back to the town. Now that we have children we've been trying to get close to the family there, but it's very difficult.

They are doing exhumations in Comalapa. When they asked for help, my wife and I went, to help look for my father-in-law, to see if we can find him, because my wife can't leave it alone. It's something she needs to do, she wants to find her father, where he is, and see him, even if he is in his bones.

When there's unfinished grief, there's no closure. So we have to keep searching for him. She's now thinking about DNA exams of the bodies. They have found more than 200 bodies in hidden graveyards. This is true. I have been there myself doing excavations, and it's horrific to see how the bodies have been thrown into the communal graves.

What I am trying to say is that the effects are long-lasting, they continue even now and, unfortunately, the government is not doing anything. It's all being done by non-govermental organizations, international ones, that are helping. According to the peace accords, the government should guarantee that the victims were helped economically, materially, and psychologically. But the government doesn't care. They are not doing it.

Víctoria and I have made the decision to tell our children the truth about what happened. I think we shouldn't be like some Guatemalans who want to hide that history. But we don't want to just tell them that it happened because the guerrilla manipulated the indigenous people and the army killed them saying that they were all guerrillas, etc. Things were not that simple. We must tell them the truth so that it doesn't happen again, so that they can, in the future, prevent it from happening again.

One of the primary functions of both the *REHMI Report* and the *CEH Report*, is "to bring those voices back to life." Merskey says the exhumations are another way that the voices have been brought back, "not in the form of words but in the remains of people, their bones, which for a forensic anthropologist actually speak in ways that sometimes words don't capture."

Eliseo, Víctoria and Ical are in their late twenties and early thirties. They have professional degrees. They have their own children. They have all the outward aspects of a successful life. In spite of their competence and successes, however, they live something of a dual life: they must balance the unresolved feelings of a bereft "inner child" with the demands and realities of adult life.

10

The Violence Within

BY THE TIME I MET WILFREDO, a young medical student, I had taken many testimonies; I thought I had a good sense of how the stories tended to unfold. But sometimes during a conversation you think you're talking about one thing, and then you realize that you're talking about that, and also about something completely different.

. . . .

"When I was seventeen or eighteen, I felt very insecure at night. I would wake up at night and cry. Even if I had to go the bathroom, I wouldn't go because I would feel that I was going to be killed or kidnapped."

—Wilfredo

WILFREDO'S WAR

Wilfredo is a 25-year-old K'iche' Maya man. He has just finished his medical studies at Centro Universitario de Occidente and is doing his residency in pediatrics.

During the worst part of the war I was about seven and eight years old. I lived in a village near Quetzaltenango with my parents. My parents were very scared. I remember they told us to

129

Wilfredo

be careful, and not go out at night. We heard the news of what was happening in Huehuetenango—that entire towns were being burned, people were killed, they were cutting open pregnant women to take the baby out--so we were very frightened.

Two people in my family suffered greatly. One of my uncles was accused of being a guerrilla. Somebody told him that the army would come to get him at home. He didn't think twice, and escaped to the mountains. I remember when they came to look for him at the house, there were many soldiers, cars, all very well armed, determined to get him. The army didn't know he'd fled and he managed to escape.

Another of my uncles was a salesman who traveled to the communities of Huehuetenango. He left the house with clothes to sell one morning, but he never returned. We don't know whether he was imprisoned or killed. We don't know anything, just that he disappeared.

My parents were very careful with each one of us. I'm the oldest of three brothers. My father used to tell us the stories when we sat down for dinner, he usually would tell us what happened in other municipalities. There were nights when we heard bombs, explosions, the sounds of rockets, and he would tell us that we had to pray to God to avoid falling into sin. When we heard those noises, we were very scared, and my father tried to calm us down saying that we had to trust in God, to relax, that it wasn't going to happen to us.

Thank God, we are all together, except for my uncle who

disappeared. My other uncle who went to Mexico came back after the war. He now has a family, and lives peacefully. Thank God, my parents and siblings are alive. In that sense, the war didn't affect us.

But personally, I think the war has affected me very much. I think I've gotten a little over it now, but when I was seventeen or eighteen, I felt very insecure at night. I would wake up at night and cry. Even if I had to go the bathroom, I wouldn't go because I would feel that I was going to be killed or kidnapped. It had such a psychological impact on me that I'm still afraid. When I hear very loud noises, I still get scared easily. Since my brothers were much younger than me at that time, I think they were less affected.

I decided to study medicine because when I was young one of my little brothers got sick with a fever, and my parents couldn't find transportation to the hospital for emergency care. So, my brother died for lack of medical care. Even then, it made me think that we needed a doctor nearby in the rural areas, where we are far from hospitals, so that people could get care at night, when they didn't have the money to pay for a taxi to take the sick person to the hospital. That motivated me to study medicine, to be able to help the people in my community. I was very enthusiastic when I first went to the university. However, my last year was very difficult economically, since my parents don't have a lot of money, and there is a certain level of family violence at home. Also, I encountered several obstacles, a lot of discrimination and racism from my classmates.

I already told you part of my motivation to choose my career. But also, six months ago, I was working in San Sebastián Coatán, a village in Huehuetenango. It struck me that there are not physicians there. I'd never been to those places, and I was surprised because people there use natural medicines to treat diseases. However, there were women and children dying because of the shortage of physicians. Some of the people who came for a consultation with a doctor had to walk for three or four hours to take a bus, and then ride for two more hours to get to the village. They would ask me to please see them right away before the bus left because, if they missed it, they wouldn't have a way to go back home. Those are the people who need medical attention the most, and that motivates me even more to keep going. I would like to specialize in pediatrics. In our country children and women are the ones with the highest death rates, and I'd like to help change that situation.

I'm still single. However, I would like to marry one day and have children. I'd tell my children what happened in our country. Those are experiences they should know as part of our history and our culture. The good part is that they will not be hurt by it as we have been. I'd try to give them a complete education, to make sure that they don't suffer all the shortages that I had. There were days when I couldn't eat, and I don't want them to suffer like that. I want them to have everything they need, so that they can move forward, be someone in this life, so that they can help others. Thank you.

Wilfredo had answered the questions systematically, as if he were taking a final exam. He was obviously a careful, conscientious student. Our interview was over. But when I thanked him, he didn't move. We sat quietly at the table, then he continued:

I have a great deal of sadness. I still feel the military is to blame for my brother's death. Maybe if the violence hadn't existed then, if it hadn't been dangerous on the streets, it's possible that my brother could have been taken to the hospital.

It's very hard for me to talk about what happened. There are many people that don't know about it. Maybe I've told a couple of my classmates, but the majority don't know. I feel that there is a lot of resentment inside me. For instance, one of my classmates told me that one of his brothers saw a soldier grab a pregnant woman, cut open her belly, and take her baby out alive. Then, as if it were a toy, he grabbed the baby hard, and threw him against the wall. The woman died from the pain and bleeding. He also told me that in his town men would appear hanging from trees, without ears, or tongue, with their sexual organs cut. They were hanged naked, sometimes putrid. He told me these things. And I think this also adds to the resentment that I feel.

With a ferocious swipe of his hand, Wilfredo brushed away a tear.

Our interview was over. We sat in silence together. Then to mark the end of our time, I shook his hand. "Gracias, Wilfredo." *I hope he knows how to take care of himself after telling me so much, being so vulnerable.*

"Wilfredo, please take care of yourself this afternoon."

But he didn't stand. He sat, staring at the floor.

"Wilfredo? Would you like to talk some more?"

I'd like to tell you something else that happened in my family. It's about family violence. There's still a lot of that in Guatemalan families. When I was about ten years old, I remember that my mother started to work making typical embroidery, because my father didn't make enough money. She went to sell it every Friday at a big market. She would take me with her and there were some days when we got delayed coming back because there wasn't a bus or we would miss our bus. When we got home late, my father would not talk, he'd just grab my mom by her hair, hit her and kick her. One day, my father broke a thermos on her head just because she had forgotten to fill it up with water. On another occasion, my father asked her how many men she had stopped to talk to on the street, and so on, and then he hit her. One time, he hit her face, her eye was swollen, bleeding. Sometimes I would intercede asking my father not to hit her, and he would scream at me, pull my hair, and kick me. Sometimes when my mom took us to church and we were late (coming home), he would hit us.

One other time, we (my brothers and I) turned the volume up on my father's radio, so he threw it to the floor and broke it. I didn't think it was such a big deal, but he broke it to pieces. Another time, we were cutting paper with scissors and by mistake we cut a little piece of our pants. He grabbed the pants, cut them completely and burned them. He would hit us and say very mean things to us. Another time, one of my brothers had broken a small mirror and my father hit him like he was a ball. When my mom tried to defend him, he hit her. Then I tried to intercede, and he hit me, too.

He wouldn't give her money for what we needed. My mother worked and tried hard to buy us food and clothing. Sometimes we would leave the house and she'd take refuge at my grandparents' house. One time, after being hit so much, she went to their house and we stayed behind with my father. He would say that it was our fault that he couldn't go to work, he would scream at me, mistreat me, and that hurt so much.

I think that all the hitting passes—it heals—but the words, the oral aggression can't be forgotten, it resonates in one's mind. Those were some of the things that happened in my home that I remember from when I was old enough to understand what was happening until I was twenty-two or twenty-three.

I think that the war had an impact on my father because in 1985 or '86, he couldn't go to work because he was afraid. I remember that he would lock the door, and also barricade it with two strong sticks so that nobody could get in. I think he must have suffered some psychological trauma.

But this situation has improved a lot since one of my brothers got married and my sister-in-law got pregnant. Since my nephew was born, my father has changed a lot. He doesn't hit us like he did before and he treats my mom better. My nephew has been a blessing, he brought peace to my home just by being born. Now my father provides money for food and clothing. He has analyzed what he did, and now he has a better attitude, despite the fact that he is still a violent man. I also think that the way he was brought up has some influence on him, because he told me that his parents were violent, aggressive, and that must have affected him.

There are many things I can not tell you, some that I remember, others that I forgot; some that are easy to tell, others are very difficult. I am grateful to you for giving me this opportunity to express some things that I remember very well that still hurt and make me afraid and leave me with deep resentments.

Wilfredo had talked until he said everything that he needed to say at this time. He stood and we took each other's hand, holding, rather than shaking.

Wilfredo relates how the violence of the world around him came inside his home, affecting his parents, his brothers and his own life. The external violence of the outside world became internalized. Héctor is another young man who talked about children and about family violence.

. . . .

"The main thing is to educate children without violence."
—Héctor

HÉCTOR'S WAR

Héctor is a 20 year old Mam Maya man studying law at the University of San Carlos. Although he doesn't have children yet, he is already thinking about the interplay of political and familial violence and its effect on children.

The people have many sequelae from the war which we can see now in the violence in our cities, mainly in the capital...

When I have children, because I don't have them yet, I will tell them the history of how things happened, because they will be the ones, when we die, that will continue in this country,

Héctor

and it depends on them that this country changes. So, if they have an understanding of what happened in our country, they'll have the social conscience to change that history, to prevent it from happening again and to help people who are still suffering the consequences. And mostly, in regards to the children that my friends have, or that I'll have someday, the main thing is to educate them without violence because when a parent is violent with their kids, he's teaching them about violence and placing the seeds for violence again in them.

Here we have heard from Wilfredo, a young man who is living

with the long-term effects of growing up in a violent home, as well as the terror of living in a war zone. He experiences pervasive fear that has been internalized, that does not disappear even after external circumstances change (the fighting ends, his father is less violent). Neither he nor Héctor have children yet, but they are both committed to ending the violence within by "not placing the seeds of violence" in the next generation.

11
Waiting for God

AND WHAT ABOUT RELIGION DURING THE VIOLENCE? In *Through a Glass Darkly: The U.S. Holocaust in Central America*, Thomas Melville calls Latin Americans "eminently religious" stating that "in the literature they produce and in the culture they live (they) are eminently, overwhelmingly folk Roman Catholic."

Melville describes the overlap between traditional religion and magical realism, that uniquely Latin American literary genre.

> (Magical realism) mirrors Latin Americans' ability to move from the cares of everyday life to levels of fantasy that make such cares, if not understandable, at least bearable. In this environment, little is what it seems and what seems to be is only a shadow of what is; dreams, beliefs, and thoughts blend together in an ever-shifting kaleidoscope of interpretations; souls/spirits and angels, good and bad, flit about...making the actual seem frivolously supernatural, all overseen and apparently approved by a nitpicking God.

Scholars of Latin American church history note that the relationship between politics and religion in Guatemala has a rich and complex history. Here, political meaning and religious meaning are deeply intertwined. At the time of the Conquest, the Maya were forced to give up their religion and to convert to Catholicism or at least pretend to do so. But for most Maya this new religion was a veneer, and ancestral patterns of worship remained a vital source of hope and meaning. Some have labeled this synchestistic blend "Christo-paganism", and it persists in Maya culture to this day. In *The Soul of Development*, Amy Sherman writes "Many villagers who call themselves Catholics are neither devout followers of these ancient Maya ways nor of Rome's. These sorts of Catholics attend Mass sporadically and baptize their children in the Catholic Church. On special occasions (before deciding on a marriage partner, for example) they may consult a Maya diviner, called a daykeeper, for advice."

During la violencia, traditional religion in Guatemala changed rapidly. In *Encountering God*, theologian Diana Eck describes how Liberation Theology challenged establishment Catholicism by calling for social action and focusing on "the Gospel as understood by the poor, the marginalized, those who speak the word of truth outside the houses of privilege and comfort...insist that our priorities be set, not by interests of the mighty, but by the priorities of the poor." The struggle between the authority of the Church and the empowerment of the faithful was played out in villages and urban slums throughout the country. Many priests and catequistas became committed to working with the poor, encouraging community participation and promoting social activism. Because of their work for social justice, they were in grave danger, often accused of being subversives or communists. Many, like Bishop Gerardi, were murdered or kidnapped. In *Paradise in Ashes*, author Beatriz Manaz quotes the U.N. Truth Commission report: there were "1,169 victims of disappearances, torture, and death among members of the church."

Theologian Susan White notes the role that Protestantism

played during this time. "Other religious options also presented themselves forcefully, options not tainted by the political marriage between the Catholic hierarchy and the repressive state. Protestants, both evangelicals and Pentecostalists, had, since the 1950s, engaged in persistent and effective missionary campaigns throughout Central and South America. At the time of the civil war, they had become a viable religious force in Guatemala. Protestantism offered the dispossessed unmediated access to the love and mercy of God, and the promise of a better future through faith in Jesus Christ. But a whole-hearted commitment, and the rejection of the convert's former life, including traditional religious practice, was expected."

The power of religion and God's blessing was invoked by all sides. In this context of little being what it seems, General Rios Montt, an evangelical Christian, oversaw the worst of the genocidal violence in the early 1980s. When he took power in 1981, he evoked a higher power: "Neither votes nor bullets gave me this position of authority; neither votes nor bullets. God placed me here." Perverting religion for his own murderous purposes, he declared, "We are able to speak politically, but we also have the ability to defend ourselves with weapons, to work with weapons, to fulfill our duty with weapons…Father, Lord, I beg you to bring peace to the heart of Guatemalans…Thank you, God, in the name of Jesus Christ. Amen."

The place of religion in the landscape of these men and women's lives is varied: some, like Carlos's widow, speak of it directly, some do not mention it at all. Some were raised Catholic, some Protestant; others, like Hélida and Mateo, have turned away from traditional Christianity to seek their Maya spiritual roots.

. . . .

"All of us, my parents and my siblings prayed together, at the same time my parents talked to us as
if they were saying their goodbyes in case we were
assassinated."

—Mateo

MATEO'S WAR

Mateo is a 30-year-old Spanish teacher who has a political and
sociological analysis of the violence. Here he remembers what happened when the army came to his highland village, how his parents
gathered their children together to pray throughout the night.

In the years 1980–82, I was seven or eight years old. It was a
very sad time for the Maya population. We lived in a village in
Huehuetenango, five or six kilometers away from the places
where the massacres of Q'anjob'al people took place...When
the military came to my town, the massacres didn't go on because the soldiers were exhausted and tired of so many innocent
peasants' deaths.

Because of the closeness of my village to the eliminated
communities, around noon people running away from the as-
sassins started passing by headed towards the nearby city. They
carried with them whatever they could, like blankets and other
light things, in a hurry, without taking into consideration the
roads. Sometimes they stopped for a few minutes and told my
parents to flee with them. However, my parents told them they
couldn't leave their home and their possessions. The whole
community waited to see what was going to happen that afternoon.

Our community was always well organized and supported
each other, so they made a decision about what to do. In order
to make clear they were not guerrilla members, the older community members decided to get together and raised a flag tied

to a stick, and forming two lines, they crossed the village and walked to meet the military around four or five in the afternoon.

They met the soldiers with the respectful greeting, then they took them to the local school building to listen to the commanding officer. Given the reception they got, the military were grateful and asked for food. Tortillas were collected and chickens were killed. By this time it was almost dark.

That night the military told the men of the community they could return in peace to their homes to rest because they were going to keep watch as that's what they had done in the other communities. When we went to bed, all of us, my parents and my siblings prayed together, at the same time my parents talked to us as if they were saying their goodbyes in case we were assassinated. We were seven children in total and I don't remember exactly whether all of us were there, but at that age I didn't understand much about what was going on, I don't remember very well, but I think I slept that night.

It was dawn; nothing happened during the night. The military left, but before they left, they organized the older men in the village, calling them *Patrullas de Autodefense Civil* (PACs) whose function was to guard the community day and night from the supposed attack by the guerrilla in different strategic places in the village. [1]

---

1. In *Guatemala: Eternal Spring, Eternal Tyranny* author Jean-Marie Simon explains that the civil patrol system was created by the military supposedly to "arm civilians against subversive incursions." In reality, the PACs "controlled a rural population the army did not trust...and gave the military a defenseless scapegoat on whom to pass off its own atrocities, either by forcing patrollers to carry out their own dirty work, or by merely claiming that alleged killings were the work of overzealous PAC units."

Mateo's parents were not willing to leave their community. All they could do was gather their children around them and pray.

During his *testimonio* a young architecture student described the importance of religion in his mother's life, how her religion saved her from despair, giving her the strength to survive tragedy that seemed insurmountable.

My mother is very Christian. Evangelical. Very, very Christian. This gave my mother strength. She says, 'God helps me, if it hadn't been for Him, anything may have happened, we even might have died.' My father was Catholic, and when I was a boy, he brought me to church. But I don't go to church now. I respect the Maya religion, but I don't believe in any of this really.

Like this mother, Balam's grandmother joined an evangelical church. He respects her choice but can not see a role for religion in his own life:

I've tried to investigate many religions. I was with Catholics, Protestants, with Jehovahs and the Mormons, but I really don't agree with many of the things they teach. I don't think there is a God that is going to send us for an eternity to Hell, for example. I was in Hell here on earth.

My grandmother is lost. She doesn't care anymore, she just wants to feel some peace. She joined the Protestants, but it's a very quiet group, they don't make noise and things, and they help each other. There are many desperate Maya women who lost everything, and they joined the evangelical church. They are helping each other in the Maya way. So it's another form of surviving. My grandmother is there, and I don't want to tell her that it's not good, I just want her to die in peace.

But I don't like religion now. The evangelicals, they are attacking the culture, they are saying we have rituals, that we come from the devil, that we are satanical. They say that we take hearts, we make sacrifices, that we are pagans. They have distorted the story of the Maya. The Maya are not like this at all.

Both of these young men were raised in a religious tradition but are no longer observant. Another student, Flor, offers a different perspective, that of an observant Catholic:

> If I could say something to my children, what I would tell them is I'm Catholic, what I mean is I have a God in my heart, and that what happened here in Guatemala during that time wasn't just, it wasn't right. But there is a justice above, and I trust in this.

Spiritual concerns and religious expression continue to have deep significance in Guatemala today. In March, 2007, President George Bush chose Iximché, a sacred Maya site, from which to give a speech about immigration of Guatemalans to the United States. Protestors gathered. After the visit, the *New York Times* quoted Jorge Morales, a protest leader, saying "Iximché represents the dignity of the Maya people and we can't have a man who represents war come to this place...Our ancestors spent hundreds of years on this ground and they will feel his presence." Juan Tiney of the Coordinating Body of Indigenous and Campesino Organizations (CONIC) added, "The presence of Bush in a place like Iximché stains the honor of this site, in light of all the deaths and pain that he has sown around the world. His entrance to these sacred lands is an affront to our culture." Protest leaders planned "a ritual cleansing of the negative energy left behind...a thorough spiritual cleaning, complete with flowers and song and dance."

In May, 2007, Pope Benedict XVI visited Latin America, where, according to the *Los Angeles Times*, he gave a speech which included the following statements: "The proclamation of Jesus and His Gospel did not at any point involve an alienation of the pre-Columbus cultures, nor was it the imposition of a foreign culture." He continued, asserting that "the people of the Americas had been silently longing" for Christ "without realizing it, and willingly received a Holy Spirit who came to make their cultures fruitful, purifying them."

In response, a representative of indigenous groups from the Quechua Indian Association declared: "Surely the Pope doesn't realize that the representatives of the Catholic Church of that era, with honorable exceptions, were complicit accessories and beneficiaries of one of the more horrible genocides that humanity has seen."

Here we have dictators who declare themselves to be righteous Christians while perpetrating massacres; a US president who chooses a sacred Maya site to give a speech, blind to the pain and anger this generates; a Pope who believes that indigenous people were yearning for Catholicism—this is indeed a world where, as Thomas Melville says, "little is what it seems and what seems to be is only a shadow of what is."

12
Peace?

The peace accords have yet to be
implemented…The government
clearly sees us as ignorant, but we
already know the contents of the
Accords. After all, we were actors
in crafting the Accords. Besides, it
is the government's job, not ours,
to read the Accords and enact
them.

—Candelaria Montejo, *Re-
port on Guatemala: Ten
Years of Peace?*

PEACE NEGOTIATIONS BEGAN in 1987 between the government and
the Guatemalan National Revolutionary Unity (URNG), but
stalled two years later. In January 1994, negotiations resumed with
the United Nations serving as the moderator, and on December 29,
1996, the Firm and Lasting Peace Accords were formally signed,
ending thirty-six years of civil war.

In her book about the peace process, *Of Centaurs and Doves,* Susanne Jonas says that, in addition to ending the armed conflict between the army and insurgents, the peace accords made provisions
to respect human rights, to provide compensation for victims, work
to end impunity and to bring human rights violators to justice. The
Guatemalan nation was to be redefined as "multiethnic, multicul-
tural, and multilingual, with a commitment to guarantee indigenous

147

rights to their diverse cultures, languages, and ideologies."

What changes has peace brought to Guatemala ten years after the accords were signed? According to the *Report on Guatemala*,

> By 2002 Amnesty International had characterized the situation in Guatemala as a "human rights melt-down…dominated by alliances between traditional sectors of the oligarchy, a transnational elite, elements of the national police, the military, and common criminals."

Candelaria Montejo, a former guerrilla fighter, is now a womens' rights advocate in Guatemala. Reflecting on the extent to which the peace accords have changed life in Guatemala she said, "One change is that in the past, those who participated in promoting the struggle were all men. Now, women participate in community struggles." But, she continued, "The peace accords have yet to be implemented. In terms of human rights, which is a key theme of the accords, it is the government's obligation…to strengthen organizations and individuals that are dedicated to ensuring that human rights are respected. On the contrary, those of us who work for human rights are accused of being obstacles to development."

When I took testimonios I did not ask specifically about the peace accords or how the country had changed since peace was declared. However, the topic was discussed by several people, including Andrés.

. . . .

"The peace that was dreamed about did not arrive."

—Andrés

ANDRÉS'S WAR

Andrés, is a 28-year-old Kaqchikel Maya man studying law at the University of San Carlos.

I think that on paper the civil war has come to an end in 1996, when the peace accords were signed. But now [2007] I don't think that they've been implemented, because the points that were agreed on, to improve the economic and political situation of the Maya...well, in a few public positions they have a few Maya, but they only have us there for the purpose of presentation. The masses of Maya should be helped, but always the people with economic power make it impossible for us to advance by putting obstacles in our path. The only thing that the peace accords have accomplished is that there has been a ceasefire between the two sides, the army and the guerrillas. The peace that was dreamed about did not arrive. You want to get to the point when you can go out in the street, without fearing anything. But it's the exact opposite. Now you go out asking God to bring you back home, today this is the fear that all the people have. One goes out without knowing if you will make it back, because delinquency is so bad, not just in the capital but all over the country.

So, in spite of the fact that the war officially ended over ten years ago, Andrés is afraid that it is still not safe to walk the streets. However, José, a young lawyer, offers a different perspective on life after the peace accords.

I remember that when I was about 6 or 7 there was always fear when the army came, and psychologically, even now, when one looks at a soldier, there is still fear...But now we can talk easily about all of that because the peace was signed, so there is not fear to talk about the conflict.

. . . .

"So once again they are dehumanizing us, only
looking at the economic side, and not at the humanity of the people."
—Laura

LAURA'S WAR

Laura, the mental health worker who gathers testimonios from
survivors, focuses on another aspect of peace, the payment of reparations if the loss of a family member can be documented:

> *And now comes along something* like the reparations, which is
> good because it is being made clear that the State was the guilty
> party, the monster behind all of this. But it continues to divide
> families, divide communities, it separates people: 'In your fam-
> ily was he disappeared or was he killed?' 'Were you able to ex-
> hume him?' 'Can you present me the death certificate as proof
> that he died?'
>
> Some money will be paid to each family, but if the person
> was 'disappeared' they'll be paid a certain amount. But I think
> it is all the same. Because people suffer when a loved one was
> 'disappeared,' just like someone suffers when a loved one was
> killed. The suffering is the same, it shouldn't have a different
> payment. This creates new divisions among the people. Once
> again there will be conflict between people in the same com-
> munity (just like during the war). Or even within the family.
> For example, if we are five surviving children, and they killed
> our dad, the five of us are going to divide the money, which is
> good because of the economic situation that the families are in.
> But for me, it doesn't make sense to my head or to my heart to
> have to divide up economically my dad or my mom. My loved
> one does not have a price.

Once again, they are making us lose our values as indigenous people. Because for us Maya, you shouldn't cut a branch from a tree without asking the tree's permission, you shouldn't cut down a tree, you shouldn't take the life from a tree without asking permission. This is true even more for people, because they are much more valuable. So if they are giving us only money they are dehumanizing us.

For me there are still many questions that remain. In the communities, when I talk with the women, they ask, 'Why did this happen to us?' I ask the same question.

Víctoria referred to the payment of reparations in her testimonio, saying that the idea that they were supposed to "compensate" families was unjust. She felt, as Laura did, that this payment of money divided communities, and even families, against one other.

Almost two decades later the stage of the so-called reconciliation is beginning…reparations for material, human, psychological, and cultural damages are to be paid. The only thing it has managed is to hand over a check for 24,000 quetzales (approximately $3,000) which is supposed to be reparation for the wrongs and losses we experienced.

The only thing that this type of action is causing is more conflict, because a mother who lost her husband receives a check for this amount and has to divide it up among the number of children she has, and also share it with the parents of the man who has disappeared or been murdered. This does not take into account the money a family has to spend to get access to this miserable amount of money, not to mention the bureaucracy or (having to deal with) the kinds of people who run this program. It some cases it creates more family divisions and conflicts because only 15% of the affected people have managed to get this so-called compensation. It is a demeaning, even humiliating situation for the affected families.

Let's not talk about the justice part of it, which is far from succeeding in making up for the wrongs or in creating an environment of peace and democracy. For many of us, twenty years or more have passed during which we suffered the consequences of a conflict that was not ours, and which continues to have repercussions in the present lives of many Maya men and women.

A decade of peace that has not been realized in everyday life; it is still not safe to walk the streets. Money that is supposed to compensate victims has resulted in humiliating families and dividing communities. On April 24, 1998, two days before he was murdered, Bishop Juan Gerardi presented the *REHMI Report*. He spoke of peace, saying:

> Peace is possible—a peace that is born from the truth that comes from each one of us and from all of us. It is a painful truth, full of memories of the deep and bloody wounds of the country. It is a liberating and humanizing truth that makes it possible for all men and women to come to terms with themselves and their life stories. It is a truth that challenges each one of us to recognize our individual and collective responsibility and commit ourselves to action so that those abominable acts never happen again.

Although the war is over, peace as envisioned in the Firm and Lasting Peace Accords is not yet a reality in Guatemala.

13

Murder in Guatemala City

VÍCTOR WAS IN THE ORIGINAL GROUP OF LANGUAGE STUDENTS. What I remember most was his radiant smile and warm handshake as he greeted each one of us with an enthusiastic, "Good morning, Teacher!" as he arrived for class. I found out later that he was known for cheering everyone on by saying, *¡Échenle ganas muchá!* (Come on, go for it!)

Later, his fiancée, Maura, told me that he was a role model for young people in his village in the Ixcán, because "he was a person who turned his suffering and problems into challenges." She added, "They really appreciate him and his talents. They want to see the same talents grow up in his young son."

But there was another side to Víctor's life. Griselda, one of his best friends, told this story:

I want to tell you something. Víctor was worried. He told me he was scared. And, you know, Víctor had problems, he drank too much, and he had a big mouth when he got mad. Víctor was traumatized from what happened to him when he was a little boy.

You know who General Gramajo is? He was one of the

153

generals during the violence. Afterwards, he gave lectures all around trying to change his (reputation and) history. Anyway, he gave a talk at the university to a class Víctor was in, and, you know Víctor, he always spoke up. He asked a lot of questions, he contradicted what Gramajo was saying. The General asked, "Who are you? What do you know about it?" and Víctor said, "I know what I'm talking about because I'm a victim of your military. You assassinated my mother," he said, before we pulled him down into his seat.

After the talk Gramajo called him over. "Who are you, what's your name?" Víctor told him, and the General said, "I like you, you stand up for what you believe".

It was after that that Víctor told us he was afraid. He wasn't sorry he said what he did, but he didn't feel safe.

On Friday August 19, 2005, Víctor was murdered in Guatemala City. When his landlady realized that he hadn't come home, she called his friends, hoping that they knew where he was. Then she did something almost unimaginable in my world, commonplace in hers. She went to look for him in the morgue.

Giovani, another of Víctor's close friends, tells what happened next.

On Monday at 8:30 in the morning, Robin, Fernando, Bartolo, and me, we went to the morgue, and when we arrived we met two cousins of Víctor's, and they told us that, regrettably, the body had been identified. It was incomprehensible that this could be true...somebody so young and with so much future, he was to have graduated this year. For many of us it continues being difficult to understand and accept, and in spite of how we try to turn the reality around, it doesn't change.

Later that day Víctor's family, two siblings, neighbors and his fiancée, Maura, arrived. Víctor also leaves a baby of eight months. He is strong and healthy, and he bears a palpable resemblance to his father. Somehow it was a very pleasant surprise to learn of the existence of this creature, amid an atmosphere of being weighed down by a very deep pain.

I had the opportunity to get to know Víctor's family. They are such strong people that, in spite of the blow, they continue to stand. It is incredible that something so painful can provide the opportunity for so many of us to realize that the most important thing is to be together. But it seems sometimes that this is the only way that we can understand it.

The legal process took a long time, but finally the morticians allowed the body to be moved. Finally at about 5:00 in the afternoon the body was released to Víctor's family. They began the trip to return back to their community, in a small village of Ixcán, north of the Quiché, 400 kilometers from Guatemala City. Bartolo and Belardo, two of the students in the program, accompanied Víctor's family.

Víctor was very delighted with the English program, and I am sure he was very grateful...All here are trying to assimilate it...but it is hard.

I read these words on a cool summer evening in northern Vermont, as far from the streets of Guatemala City as I could be. Somehow, I felt like my heart was separated from my body, beating in a different country.

Griselda said, "Some people have said they believe that Víctor was a victim of street crime, that it was a robbery that got out of hand. Sure, it's possible. But Víctor was poor, he didn't have anything. Gang violence? Maybe it was just random. Maybe."

14

A Flame Inside Us

THEY SURVIVED THE VIOLENCE, THE HORROR, AND THE TRAUMA. But what does the future hold for these young survivors? In so many of the testimonios I heard that unspoken question: "What pieces of a shattered past can I reclaim to take with me as I continue to live my life?" The answers, varied as they were, always had to do with connecting: with their culture, with their people, with the past. In fact, in every conversation each person spoke in their own words about their commitment to maintaining Maya identity and to working for their Maya communities. This is what Juan Carlos calls "the flame inside," a flame that empowers them to move forward while staying connected to their ancient tradition. And, most importantly, this commitment is a way to honor the dead and the disappeared. Carmen says simply, "We have to continue fighting for justice for the family and the community since that was the job my father started."

. . . .

"They kidnapped my father, he disappeared, and, to this date, we don't know anything about him, whether or not he died. After this, my older siblings had no other option but to join the guerrillas."

—Carmen

CARMEN'S WAR

Carmen is a 25-year-old K'iche' Maya woman finishing her degree in environmental engineering at Universidad Rural de Guatemala.

My name is Carmen. I was just a few weeks old when my whole family had to leave Santa Cruz del Quiché for the capital. My father was a health provider in the town, and he was very involved with religious activities, so my father and three older siblings were on the army's "black list." My mother wasn't, but they decided that we all should go to the capital to be safer.

Then, from around 1980, 1981, we lived in the city. My father had to start working selling fruits and vegetables. My older brothers also helped him, while my mother stayed home with us, the younger ones, and took care of the house. We hadn't been in the capital very long when my grandparents on my father's side, and a cousin, were massacred in Santa Cruz del Quiché.

A few months later, they kidnapped my father. He disappeared, and, to this date, we don't know anything about him, whether or not he died. After this, my older siblings had no other option but to join the guerrillas. Three of them joined, and one of them had to go into exile in Mexico. The four younger ones stayed with my mother. One of my sisters that joined the guerrillas got pregnant and had to come back to the capital to live with us. She started doing my father's job, selling vegetables. We never stayed very long at one place, we moved constantly. One week in one place, a few days in another. My mother constantly heard news that the army wanted to kill our whole family. So, she decided to leave my two young brothers in a boarding school. They were there for about ten years. My younger sister and I were left at another boarding school. We were there for almost four years.

My mother worked with an organization for people who

had been displaced during the war. For several years she was an activist there. Then, she decided she had to get us four younger siblings together again, and she came back and got my sister and me, but my other two young brothers were left at the boarding school.

After many years, when the peace was signed, I met my older siblings. I only recently met them. They came back from the mountains to 'normal' life, so to say. I think that may be why we aren't close as a family. Each one is doing their own thing.

However, we all know we have to continue fighting for justice for the family and the community since that was the job my father started in Santa Cruz del Quiché. That's all I have to say.

. . . .

> "I believe that when people are the victims of something like what we have suffered, there is always a mark left, but I try to be positive. I don't hate the army, but I ask them to apologize, to ask for forgiveness, to see if I can forgive them."
>
> —Juan Carlos

JUAN CARLOS'S WAR

Juan Carlos is also committed to fighting for justice. He is a 25-year-old Uspanteko Maya man in his fifth year of studying law at the University of San Carlos. His father disappeared in 1982; Juan Carlos never knew him.

My name is Juan Carlos. I was born in the Quiché Department, which was one of the areas more affected by the political conflict in Guatemala. At the beginning of the '80s, exactly on May 11, 1982, my father was kidnapped by the army. From that date on, I don't know anything about him. When I was about ten, someone came to my house and confessed that he

Juan Carlos

had taken part in my father's kidnapping and from what he said, I have an idea of where he (the body) might be. Supposedly, he died at the army camp. There have been three excavations there, but they haven't found any bodies, in spite of the fact that this person said my father had been killed and buried there.

I grew up with my grandfather, my mother's father. Ever since I was little, he was clear with me about what had happened to my father. They never lied to me, they always told me my father was dead. They didn't explain why or how, but I understood it when I grew up. I think that made me more mature, with some difficulties, though. For example, when I was at school, it was hard for me when there was a parents' meeting and my father wasn't there. We had to leave Uspantán, to search for a safe place. I grew up in Cobán, a different place than where I was born and that affected me. Many times, there is a lack of a sense of belonging because one doesn't really know where to belong. And we didn't have a stable place. There is that fear still, at least for my mother, living with that constant threat, that if my father was kidnapped, there was a reason for it. I think it has left a fear in my mother about what could happen to us.

It really affected me not to have a father. Fortunately, I had a very good mother, and I even tell her she was a good 'father', too, because she helped me get ahead, first for myself, for my family, and in my father's memory. Because my father had many dreams he couldn't live. If I could tell a story, that will be the one.

I believe that when people are the victims of something like what we have suffered, there is always a mark left, but I try to be positive. I don't hate the army, but I ask them to apologize, to ask for forgiveness, to see if I can forgive them. But, no matter what I lived through, I know that I will never have a father figure, I don't know how children see their father, because I did not have one.

But there are other good things I have gained from these experiences. For instance, I have friends whose fathers have disappeared and their bodies haven't been found, and I notice that they are sensitive to the injustice that happens to others. It made us have a deep sense of solidarity.

I think that after what we lived through, there is a willingness to study, to gain the tools to prevent the same injustices from happening to others. I studied law for that reason. I want to work for justice. Guatemala is a very unfair country. No matter where you look, there are injustices happening. It's terrible, but it's true. What I went through was about 25 years ago and this country must change. That's why we are studying, and there is a flame inside us that inspires us to be supportive.

I think it's important that we share not only our stories, but that we become united because, even though people are so good in Guatemala, the government is very bad. I think it's the only country in the world where the killer is recognized and rewarded over the victim. The memory of the people who died is not treated with dignity, which is terrible and stupid. But I think that if we were united, we could do a better job of honoring and dignifying the memory of those who disappeared. I ask that the body of my father appear, that Giovani's father and Eliseo's mother appear, or that we at least find out how they died.

Of course, when I have children, I'll tell them what happened to me. First, in my father's memory, and secondly, because Guatemala is a country that has suffered a lot, but the

people are fighters, and they are very resilient. Pain and suffering is a daily happening. And it's important that we give our
children a different Guatemala. That's what I have to say, and I
thank you for allowing me to tell the story.

. . . .

In one way or another each person sought to make meaning
out of seemingly meaningless devastation, focusing on what they
considered positive aspects that grew out of personal and cultural
tragedy. Carmen and Juan Carlos articulate some of these "good
things:" a commitment to work for justice, a deep solidarity, a flame
inside that "inspires us to be supportive."

15
What Good Does Talking Do?

"Terror silences its victims, installing generalized fear. Torture, disappearance, and murder are then denied or treated by those in power as if they did not occur. They are redefined as deaths from 'common crime.' Victims are urged to 'forget the past' so that the future may be more rapidly constructed. Traumatic events that have undermined the very existence of thousands of human beings thereby receive no social validation, thus restricting the social reality in which these events occur to private memories."

—M. Brinton Lykes

"One time at the university, I tried to talk about this, and everyone laughed at me. They said, 'You've seen too many movies.' After that I closed up and never told another thing, but today I want to do it."

—Flory

All my life I had believed in "the talking cure." After the group meeting when I first heard testimonios, I had been certain when I told Eliseo that "telling (his) story would get the poison out" of him, was absolutely true. But these stories were filled with such extreme horror that now I had started asking myself: *Is it better to talk about these horrifying memories, or better to keep them buried?* I asked the students this same question.

At the first meeting when the students gave their testimonios, Flor had been sitting next to Fernando. When he finished talking, she put her hand on his shoulder and said, "Fernando is my best friend, and today I have heard things he never told me before."

．．．．．．．

"After everything returned to being calm and normal, a huge fear stayed with us always, that one day, the same thing would happen again."
—Flor

FLOR'S WAR

Flor is a 25-year-old Kaqchikel Maya woman in her final year studying law at the University of San Carlos.

My name is Flor. I was born in 1982, in San Juan Sacatepéquez, near the capital city. Well, my father suffered. He was someone who was very active in our community and during the years '82 and '83, they wanted to kill him. There were people in my village who had a list of people's names, and my father's name was on it. Some cards arrived at our house that said that my father was going to die!

My parents didn't know what to do, with four kids already, where were they going to go? We didn't have money. My father considered going to live in the Petén, a place very far from where we lived, to hide. But he didn't want to go, he was very involved with doing a lot of projects with the Church.

One time he was hidden in the house. We lived in a very small house, including a part that had been excavated so that my father could hide. And my siblings never, ever could go out.

We were always enclosed. And all of this has come to affect us very much.

My mother is…that is, she got sick from everything that had happened. And, after everything returned to being calm and normal, a huge fear stayed with us always, that one day, the same thing would happen again. But it never did.

When I finished primary school, my father didn't want me to continue studying, and this was very hard for me, because I always liked to study. But he said, 'No, what for? Some day this fear could return, one day the same thing could happen. It's better that you follow the example of your mother who is a tranquil person, nothing ever happens to her.'

But, in spite of what he says, I want to change, I want to move ahead, to rise above this, and to be able to help if someday the same thing happens. I want to be someone who can defend our rights. This is what influenced me to study law. Now I am in the fifth year of the law program.

All children should know what happened during that time. There are books that say this, but to hear it from someone is totally different. It's not something one can read.

I want to salute my companions that experienced all of this, I am very sorry that this happened to you, but *anímate!* (take heart!) Here we are, and we have to move forward.

· · · · · · ·

Flor echoes the importance of communicating to the younger generation about what it was like growing up during the civil war. Hearing the stories is even more important than reading about them in books. But what is the effect on the person doing the telling? Does talking help relieve some of the pain by creating a community of witnesses? Or does describing the anguish bring it back, erasing any hope for the future?

What good, then, does talking do?

María: "I think it's important (to talk) because I didn't tell my mother what I saw. And during those years when I was six or seven, I was always afraid. I grew up very different than my brothers because they hadn't seen what I saw. Then, after I talked to my mother, I felt much better, and it's very important because it's a way of venting your feelings. It's a way to learn that others feel what I felt, that it's not just me, and it helps you feel understood."

Juan Carlos: "Many times I wonder why this happened to me. But it's important to know that there are people who went through the same things. I talk about it only with my friends, for instance, Giovani and Eliseo. I felt a certain affinity with them, and when we talk that feeling of solidarity emerges when they tell me their story. I feel a bond with them, because they understand when I act in a certain way. Sometimes, when I'm introverted and can't express what I'm really feeling, they understand better than other people who have not lived through the same experiences. Giovani tells me that there are many things in our lives that are similar. The fear—keeping quiet about things because in our families they taught us that—for instance, if your father died because he said what he thought, you don't do it. You keep quiet, many times for survival. But it's important to share it."

Carmen: "Sometimes we can talk about what happened, and many times we joke that when we are making a lot of money, we will go to a psychologist. Because we were born healthy, but with everything that has happened to us, we are hurt and we need therapy. We were just joking, but I do think it would be a good way to recover from the trauma. We are distrustful after what we suffered."

Juan Carlos: "Many of us think the victims are the people whose relatives were killed, but I think that everybody who lived during that time is a victim. Because there is fear, being afraid to talk, to say what we think, to exercise our rights. We were all victims when our basic human rights were taken away."

Flory: "Currently I am studying for a master's degree in mental health, I have been meeting with lots of people who still have never talked. Just touching a little bit on this topic provokes a series of cries, anguish, desperation. There is still fear, and when they see police or a soldier, immediately they feel a shiver which they associate with the pain, and they suffer again."

Laura: "There is a lot of work to be done with the young people, because many programs and projects have been offered to adult women or men, but not to the young people. I think it is important to do it (talk about what happened) because we are young people who haven't shared our experiences or we haven't found those spaces, or they don't want to listen to us, thinking that we don't have anything to say because we didn't live it, when, in fact, we did live it. So that is a challenge for us right now, how to implement space to be able to listen to these young people, so that they can also begin their catharsis. If we do this that will be a small step toward constructing a different Guatemala, not forgetting about the adults, but also listening to the stories of the young people."

In *Disappeared: A Journalist Silenced*, Viana Maza Charvarría, a niece of Irma Flaquer the famous Ladina journalist kidnapped in 1980, speaks for all young people of Guatemala who were children during the violence. She writes of a "double task:"

> We are the children of war. We are the sons and daughters of this quantity of evil that drowned our country for such a long time. It is not easy. I imagine it was not easy to live during the war, but we now have a double task. We have a bitterness that is very difficult to manage. It is something that we have learned, but at the same time, we do not feel it directly.

Juan Carlos: "I think it's important to be a channel for other generations, so that what happened in Guatemala is not forgotten. My experience, and many others, must not be forgotten. I think we should always tell it. Even though it hurts sometimes to tell it, it's also a relief. And aside from that, I think it's important that the young people now that didn't live through the armed conflict, people who come now to Guatemala and don't see guns, don't hear shots every night, that don't have to get on the ground to sleep because of fear of bullets, they have to know about it, too. They should know it was an ugly, dark time, and they should fight to prevent it from happening again."

Ical: "It is difficult to talk about these things, and in my wife's case, she couldn't talk about it for a long time. When she remembered she still couldn't talk. That's why I say that healing from the past isn't just to invite people to reclaim their things. No, it requires specialized psychological help, that really comprehends the situation. Because we've seen some organizations trying to give psychological support, but they don't really understand our people, the dimension of the problem that our people, very poor people, suffered, and the help they provide is not what people need. It's not just to say 'don't cry.' It isn't simply not to cry, but also to understand what happened and feel that pain, like we say in our Maya culture, to feel the others' pain. That's very difficult."

. . . .

"There are things that have happened that broke apart our history, the scars will never be erased, never, never, but they can be overcome."
—Flory

FLORY'S WAR

I am the oldest of 7 children. There were so many things going on in my family we didn't know what path to take. I chose to study psychology, so I could understand many things...the hatred, the anger. There was lots of alcoholism, as much for those who were victims as for those who were the victimizers, because they also were victims. Because the one who participated in the scorched earth policy, or torturing people is still a victim. They still have those memories of what happened, so they are drowning themselves in alcohol.

I did my university thesis on emotional disequilibriums of widowed women. I took testimonials and that was very difficult. When I was working on my thesis I looked for a bibliography, but when I did a comparative analysis of what I experienced and what it says in the books, it doesn't match up. Some books are written by foreigners, but they don't capture the essence. The people who wrote those books aren't able to understand the realities of the war.

When I did my thesis I came to understand that the purpose of the war is to exterminate the indigenous people. This really hurt me, because those who were in the military were indigenous people; they recruited all of the young people who weren't even 18 years old, they gave them weapons, they prepare them to go and fight. And who made up the other side? They were also young indigenous people, groups that were fleeing into the mountains to save their lives. They were victims, they were all victims. And they tried to exterminate us in that way.

For the indigenous woman it is harder for her than for the men to move forward, to reclaim her values, her principles, her customs. Her identity has been stolen and reclaiming it has been very difficult. But they are putting forth their efforts. As one lady said to me, 'I am going to take this with me to the grave. I am going to die with this, with my pain.' She counts how old her child who died would be. Others grieve over the deaths of grandparents, or great-grandparents who died when they were not that old.

There is a lot of ignorance on the part of the young people of what happened. We are trying to help the families integrate the experience, we are collecting testimonies, we are healing wounds, but we also have to conscious that this is not going to happen from one day to the next.

Flory asked us to stand and take the hand of the person next to us. We stood, and then she spoke into the silence, invoking the wisdom of the ancestors: "Thank you very much for this very special day, and also I give thanks that the grandfathers and the grandmothers gave us this opportunity to be able to talk about life, in the past, present, and future. I hope that their wisdom always accompanies us and that we can now make a network of those of us who are here to be able to keep sharing many (other) things that perhaps we couldn't share today. I thank you with all of my heart for this space."

So, what good is talking? In *Trauma and Recovery*, Judith Herman emphasizes the "restoration of social bonds" which begins with the discovery that one is not alone. Nowhere is this experience more immediate, powerful, or convincing than in a group.

> Because traumatized people feel so alienated by the experience survivor groups have a special place in the recovery process...The encounter with others who have undergone similar trials dissolves feelings of isolation, shame, and stigma.

Trauma survivors use their own language. This is Juan Carlos's simple, unadorned answer: "It is a good beginning to share our stories...Even though it hurts sometimes to tell it, it's also a relief." And this is Flor's: "I didn't know many of your stories and the truth is that, yes, I feel like I've gotten to know you at a different level...I think there is much companionship in this group sharing, learning about our different situations. I think that it is very valuable." This was said over and over in different words, in unique voices.

Hearing other people's stories helps you feel less alone. It helps to talk.

16
The Fight Against Forgetting

DURING THE EARLY DAYS OF THAT FIRST TRIP in 2004, we all heard Fernando when he said, "I am a survivor of the Guatemala civil war." Since that time I have made several trips to Guatemala and heard many people tell their stories. People have asked—and sometimes I've asked myself—why I felt I had to return. In reality, I did not feel I had chosen to do this work; it was as if Guatemala had actually chosen me.

Part of it, certainly, was being Jewish. The Cuban-American Jewish writer, Achy Obeja, describes certain Jews who are "afflicted with a feverish kind of racial memory that compels us to constantly glance backward." I came, witness to another genocide.

And, as a survivor of sexual abuse, I'd lived the survivor's history of being silenced. For years I had been afraid to tell the truth, believing that it was emotionally dangerous, that by speaking out I might lose people I loved. This is certainly not the same kind of danger that my Maya friends lived with, but it was enough to inject a particular sensitivity in my bones. I came, also, with my long history as a listener, as a believer in the redemptive power of telling the stories of our own lives. And, as I grew to understand the depth of my country's involvement in the murder of a people, I came as an

American, bearing partial responsibility for what had been done in America's name. In an interview, Jennifer Harbury put it this way:

> If we are allowing torture, then...we, as citizens of the United States, are every bit as responsible for what happens as the citizens of Germany were during the Third Reich. We are responsible for what our government does if we don't take action. We have to take action. It's our government. It's our responsibility.

But I hadn't recognized any of this when I returned to Guatemala that first time. I didn't dwell on personal motivation. I told myself that I was on a compelling intellectual quest, simply seeking to answer the question: Can there be hope in the aftermath of genocide?

In her study of resilient adults, Gina Higgins states,

> Denial of abuse abounds...for those who can tolerate bearing witness to trauma's *full* catastrophe to help the hurt heal, it is just as essential to honor the history of *hope* in their lives...Where was the light in this darkened life?...The dark and the light need to be resurrected in equal measure to help people heal.

Flory describes this profound sense of despair as a kind of physical darkness: "We felt that the nights were so long. I remember that passage as dark, very dark, like there wasn't any light. In fact, there wasn't any electricity, we just used candles. I see it as a tunnel without an exit. Without any exit at all."

Darkness, pain, and terror dominate these stories. In spite of tragedy, however, there is also a fighting spirit, a commitment to facing the past, to telling the truth, to making connections with other survivors. This is the light that Higgins refers to. This is *tikkun olom*, the idea embedded in Judaism that we each have an individual responsiblity to "repair the world." Flory tells us, "The struggle is huge, not just for us who are living in this moment but also for the generation that comes after us and for those that aren't even born yet. There are things that have happened that broke apart our history. The scars will never be erased—never, never—but they can be overcome."

In *Disappeared: A Journalist Silenced*, Viana Maza Chavarría, the young Guatemalan who described her generation as "the children of war," offers a vision of a changing society, describing a new Guatemala:

> I have a group of friends. The group is made up of the son of a military man, the son of a guerrilla commander, the daughter of an exiled couple, the son of some hippies, the daughter of someone who didn't have the least idea that there had been a war in Guatemala—that is, a bunch of children of people who couldn't even stare each other in the face. I think this is a beautiful thing…I think that things are changing and if they have not changed, they are about to change and we want them to change. We are getting there, and I think it will be easier with your help.

Elie Wiesel, the eminent scholar and Holocaust survivor, reminds us that hope is "the most vital element of all human equations."

· · · · · ·

In conclusion, the students express their hopes and dreams for the future, for themselves, for their children, and for Guatemala.

BARTOLO, LAW STUDENT

"What is most important is for us to rise above what happened, to be professionals now. I think that we are going to be the ones who make the difference in the future."

ELISEO, LAW STUDENT AND NEW FATHER

"I will be a responsible father, I don't want my child to miss the affection of a father. I want my child to be a good person, and when he grows up, I will tell him of my past so that he can reflect and appreciate life and learn how to respect the rights of everyone in the world."

RIGOBERTO, LAWYER:

"I think that the new generations should know the history of Guatemala. I will tell them of the suffering of the war, including the peace accords. Not only as the father of the family do I have the obligation to tell my kids this, but also as a professional. Because they should know it so that they don't fall into making the same mistake."

ICAL, PROJECT COORDINATOR FOR A NON-GOVERNMENTAL AGENCY:

"My wife and I have made the decision to tell our children the truth about what happened...But we don't want to just tell them that it was because the guerrillas manipulated the indigenous people and the army killed them...Things were not that simple. We must tell them the truth so that it doesn't happen again."

CARMEN, ENVIRONMENTAL ENGINEERING STUDENT:

"We all know we have to continue fighting for justice for the family and the community since that was the job my father started."

FLOR, LAW STUDENT:

"I want to change, I want to move ahead, to rise above this, and to be able to help if someday the same thing happens. I want to be someone who can defend our rights."

ANDRÉS, LAW STUDENT:

"I keep studying because, even if I'm never well-off, intellectual growth is what you put into it. You learn to think better, and do things better. You begin to be able to change yourself, and later to collaborate with the community, which really needs it."

NATALIO, LAW STUDENT:

"I have my secrets, but I haven't told them. I think that my wounds haven't healed after all that happened to me, I think I will talk about it later...I would like to learn English and study for a masters degree in Criminal Law to be able to help those that can't defend themselves. This is my vision and I will keep fighting."

FERNANDO, LAW STUDENT:

"I want to tell you that on the 7th of September of this year, it will be 22 years since my sister Bernadina was kidnapped in Guatemala City. This happened when she was 23 years old, she would be 45 now. We still have not found her. We are still waiting for her and for many others. There is no doubt her spirit will make us fight against forgetting."

VÍCTOR JOSÉ PÉREZ PABLO, INTERNATIONAL RELATIONS STUDENT, MURDERED AUGUST 2005:

"I believe in keeping the history alive, that we must confront the authoritarianism of the State. We must confront what they did, and look for a solution."

· · · · · · ·

I wanted to give the students a gift, something to acknowledge their spirit, their resilience, what they had taught me. It was impossible to imagine that I would be able to find words to express my profound gratitude and respect. Then, browsing in a bookstore the day before I was to leave, I found a poem by the K'iche' Maya poet,

Humberto Ak'abal.

And Nobody Sees Us

The flame of our blood burns
inextinguishable
in spite of the wind of centuries

We do not speak,
our songs caught in our throats,
misery with spirit,
sadness inside fences.

Ay, I want to cry screaming!

The lands they leave for us
are the mountain slopes,
the steep hills:
little by little the rains wash them
and drag them to the valleys
that are no longer ours.

Here we are
standing on roadsides
with our sight broken by a tear...

And nobody sees us.

Y Nadie Nos Ve

La llama de nuestra sangre arde,
inapagable
a pesar del viento de los siglos.

Callados,
canto ahogado,
miseria con alma,
triesteza acorralada.

Ay, quiero llorar a gritos!

Las tierras que nos dejan
son las laderas,
las pendientes:
los aguaceros poco a poco las lavan
y las arrastran a las planadas
que ya no son de nosotros.

aquí estamos
parados a la orilla de los caminos
con la mirada rota por una lágrima...

Y nadie nos ve.

A poem, someone else's words, captured the essence of what I wanted to say. And a photograph because, as I was leaving the store, my eye caught a postcard with a photograph entitled *Encuentro de Dos Mundos, 1492–1992*. Standing facing each other are Maya women and children confronting an impenetrable line of Guatemalan police. The police are in full battle gear holding clubs and shields. The women's hands are empty, except for one mother who clutches her daughter as the girl leans back into her mother's body seeking safety.

This poem, this photograph, would have to express everything

Encuentro de Dos Mundos, 1492–1992 by photographer
Daniel Hernández-Salazar

that was in my heart: gratitude, respect, solidarity.

Could anyone stay the same having witnessed the courage it takes to speak in spite of having been taught that silence is safety? Could anyone stay the same having seen the raw strength that compelled these survivors to tell their personal histories when everything would have them believe that revealing the truth is to risk disaster?

And what of that naive, young American girl on the plane whose question lent its name to this book? She had been safe, living her life, ignorant of the genocide being perpetrated around her. Just as I had been.

Guatemala changed me. Hearing these testimonios taught me that there isn't one single answer to the question, "What war?" There are as many answers as the heroic Guatemalans who trusted me with their war, and the countless others who can no longer speak.

Bibliography

Afflitto, Frank M. and Jesilow, Paul. *The Quiet Revolutionaries, Seeking Justice in Guatemala*. Austin, Texas: University of Texas Press, 2007.

Agger, I. and Jensen, S.B. "Testimony as Ritual and Evidence in Psychotherapy for Political Refugees," *Journal of Traumatic Stress* 3 (1990),1990.

Ak'abal, Humberto. *Poems I Brought Down from the Mountain*. Saint Paul, MN: Nineties Press, 1999.

Arandi, Galindo and Luis, Jorge. *Aventuras 3: Medio Social*. Guatemala: Editorial Santillana, 2006.

Burgos, Elisabeth. *I, Rigoberta Menchu; An Indian Woman in Guatemala*. London: Verso, 1983.

Clifton, Lucille. *Blessing the Boats, New and Selected Poems 1988–2000*. Rochester, NY: BOA Editions, Ltd, 2000.

Durbin, Alexandra, ed. *Report on Guatemala, Volume 28*, Number 1, Spring 2007.

Goldman, Francisco. *The Long Night of White Chickens*. New York: Grove Press, 1992.

Eck, Diana L. *Encountering God: A Spiritual Journey from Bozeman to Banaras*. Boston, MA: Beacon Press, 1993.

Erlick, June Carolyn. *Disappeared: A Journalist Silenced: The Irma Flaquer Story*. Emeryville, CA: Seal Press, 2004.

Figley, Charles. (editor). *Trauma and Its Wake*. New York: Brunner/Mazel, 1985.

Gonzales, Ramelia. *Hilos Rompiendo El Silencio, Historias Sobre Las Mujeres de la CPR-Sierra de la Guerra Civil en Guatemala*. Antigua, Guatemala: Editorial La Copian Fiel, 2005.

Gramaso, Héctor Fernando Reyes. *Estudios Sociales 7*. Guatemala: Editorial Santillana, 2006.

Commission for Historical Clarification. *Guatemala, Memory of Silence, Report of the Commission for Historical Clarification Conclusions and Recommendations*. Guatemala.

Human Rights Office, Archdiocese of Guatemala. *Guatemala, Never Again!: The Official Report of the Human Rights Office, Archdiocese of Guatemala, Recovery of Memory Project (REHMI)*. Maryknoll, NY: Orbis Books, 1999.

Harbury, Jennifer. *Bridge of Courage: Life Stories of the Guatemalan Compañeros and Compañeras*. Monroe, ME: Common Courage Press, 1994.

Harbury, Jennifer. *Searching for Everado, A Story of Love, War, and the CIA in Guatemala*. New York: Warner Books, 1997.

Herman, Judith Lewis, M.D. *Trauma and Recovery*. New York: Basic Books, 1992.

Higgins, Gina O'Connell. *Resilient Adults: Overcoming a Cruel Past.* San Francisco, CA: Jossey-Bass, 1994.

Jonas, Susanne. *Of Centaurs and Doves: Guatemala's Peace Process.* Boulder, CO: Westview Press, 2000.

The Just Word. The Ignacio Martin-Baro Fund for Mental Health and Human Rights, Spring 2000.

Lowell, George. *A Beauty That Hurts: Life and Death in Guatemala.* Austin, TX: University of Texas Press, 1995, 2000.

Lykes, M. Brinton. "Terror, Silencing and Children: International, Multidisciplinary Collaboration with Guatemalan Maya Communities". *Social Science and Medicine*, 38 (4), 1994.

Lykes, M. Brinton, with Ana Caba Mateo, Jacinta Chavez Anay, Ana Laynez Caba, Ubaldo Ruiz, and Joan Williams. "Telling Stories—Rethreading Lives: Community Education, Women's Development and Social Change Among the Maya Ixil." *International Journal of Leadership in Education, Theory and Practice*, vol 2, No 3, 1992.

Mahony, Liam and Eguren, Luis Enrique. *Unarmed Bodyguards, International Accompaniment for the Protection of Human Rights.* West Hartford, CT: KuMarían Press, 1997.

Manz, Beatriz. *Paradise in Ashes: A Guatemalan Journey of Courage, Terror, and Hope.* Berkeley: University of California Press, 2004.

Maslow, Jonathan Evan. *Bird of Life, Bird of Death: A Naturalist's Journey Through a Land of Political Turmoil.* New York: Simon and Schuster, 1986.

Voices and Images: Mayan Ixil Women of Chajul. Guatemala City, Víctor Herrera de Magna Terra editors, 2000

Melville, Thomas. *Through a Glass Darkly: The U.S. Holocaust in Central America.* Xlibris Corporation, 2005.

Melville, Thomas and Lykes, M. Brinton in *Handbook of Action Research, Participative Inquiry and Practice.* London: SAGE Publications, 2001.

Mersky, Marcie. *History As An Instrument of Social Reparation: Reflections on an Experience in Guatemala.* April 9, 1997.

Mersky, Marcie. from weblog entitled P.O.V found at the following URL: www.pbs.org/pow/pov203/discoveringdominga/special_witnessmm.html.

Miller, Robert. "Not Quite a Papal Mea Culpa." *Los Angeles Times,* May 24, 2007.

Moeller, John. *Our Culture Is Our Resistance: Repression, Refuge and Healing in Guatemala.* New York: powerHouse Books, 2004.

Montejo, Víctor. *Testimony: Death of a Guatemalan Village.* Willimantic, CT: Curbstone Press, 1987.

Obejas, Achy. *Days of Awe.* New York: Ballantine Books, 2001.

Ortiz, Sister Dianna. *The Blindfold's Eyes: My Journey from Torture to Truth.* Maryknoll, NY: Orbis Books, 2002.

Link, Matthew. *The Out Traveler,* Summer 2007. "Gore Vidal's Navigations."

Perera, Víctor. *Rites: A Guatemalan Boyhood.* San Diego, CA: Harcourt Brace Jovanovich, 1986.

Perera, Víctor. *Unfinished Conquest: The Guatemala Tragedy.* Berkeley, CA: University of California Press, 1993.

Reason, Peter and Bradbury, Hilary. *Handbook of Action Research, Participative Inquiry and Practice.* London: SAGE Publications, 2001.

Report on Guatemala, Ten Years of Peace? A Publication of the Network in Solidarity with the People of Guatemala (NISGUA) Volume 27, Number 4, Winter 2006.

Rutenberg, Jim and Lacey, Marc. "Bush Meets Anger Over Immigration Issue as He Promotes Free Trade in Guatemala." *New York Times*, March 12, 2007.

Sanford, Víctoria. *Buried Secrets: Truth and Human Rights in Guatemala.* New York: St Martin's Press, 2003.

Schlesinger, Stephen and Kinzer, Stephen. *Bitter Fruit: The Untold Story of the American Coup in Guatemala.* New York: Anchor Books, 1983.

Schirmer, Jennifer. *The Guatemalan Military Project: A Violence Called Democracy.* Philadelphia, PA: University of Pennsylvania Press, 1998.

Schwantes, David. *Guatemala: A Cry from the Heart.* Minneapolis, MN: Health Initiatives Press, 1990.

Sherman, Amy L. *The Soul of Development: Biblical Christianity and Economic Transformation in Guatemala.* New York, Oxford University Press, 1997.

Silverman, Adam. "Memory is the Soul of History". *Burlington Free Press*, April 26, 2007 (Elie Weisel quote in article).

Simon, Jean-Marie. *Guatemala: Eternal Spring, Eternal Tyranny.* New York: W.W. Norton & Company, 1987.

Steltzer, Ulli. *Health in the Guatemalan Highlands.* Seattle: University of Washington Press, 1983.

Stoll, David. *Rigoberta Menchu and the Story of All Poor Guatemalans.* Boulder, CO: Westview Press, 1999.

Vigil, María López. *Revista*. "A Train Ride Through Memory and History," October, 2006.

Weil, Simone. *The Need for Roots: Prelude to a Declaration of Duties Toward Mankind*. New York: Harper & Row, 1952.

Wilkinson, Daniel. *Silence on the Mountain: Stories of Terror, Betrayal and Forgetting in Guatemala*. Durham, NC: Duke University Press, 2004.

Wright, Ronald. *Time Among the Maya: Travels in Belize, Guatemala, and Mexico*. New York: Weidenfeld and Nicolson, 1989.

Wright, Ronald. *Stolen Continents: 500 Years of Conquest and Resistance in the Americas*. Boston, MA: Houghton Mifflin Company, 1992.

. . . .

ADDITIONAL PERMISSIONS

About the Author

Laurie Levinger went to Guatemala in 2004 as a volunteer to teach English. When one of her students introduced himself as a survivor of the Guatemalan civil war, she realized she had more to learn than to teach. She is a retired clinical social worker who has traveled to Guatemala many times to collect testimonies from Maya survivors. Her background in listening helped her hear these poignant stories, stories that are filled with tragedy, but also with hope.